Discipleship

*The Life That Cherishes
the Preeminence of Christ*

R L COURSEY

WESTBOW
PRESS®
A DIVISION OF THOMAS NELSON
& ZONDERVAN

WestBow Press books may be ordered through booksellers or by contacting:

WestBow Press
A Division of Thomas Nelson & Zondervan
1663 Liberty Drive
Bloomington, IN 47403
www.westbowpress.com
844-714-3454

ISBN: 978-1-9736-2009-9 (sc)
ISBN: 978-1-9736-2008-2 (e)

Print information available on the last page.

WestBow Press rev. date: 10/17/2023

CONTENTS

PART I

DEPRAVITY:

The Essence of the Consumer Nature

PART II

DELIVERANCE:

Allured by the Brightness of His glory

PART III

DISCIPLESHIP:

The Life that Cherishes the Preeminence of Christ

INTRODUCTION

In the Fall of 2017, I listened to a sermon where the preacher laid out in detail the story of Elijah. As the story went on, I thought, "I know this story well." "Maybe I could even tell it better." Certainly, there were too many character flaws surrounding the life of Elijah to challenge anyone's insecurity. And as for the prophets of Baal, well, they can make even the most foolish appear wise. And then, as unassuming David flung his stone, killing the laughing giant, he flung his stone on an unexpected audience who were likewise laughing at the foolishness of the prophets of Baal. And what was this unexpected stone in his arsenal? The insinuation that in many ways we may be just as foolish as the prophets of Baal. "But wait a minute," I thought, "compare us to the prophets of Baal?" I've always compared myself with the hero of the story. And, in Elijah's case, maybe I would have acted a little better. Isn't it unamerican to compare the audience with the villain of the story? In America no one is supposed to lose. Or maybe the truth is that I've never read the story thru anything but my American eyes of "me first." Maybe I need to see the story from God's perspective. Maybe I didn't know the story after all.

The lesson I gleaned from the sermon was not whether Baal worship is applicable to the church today, but what should our response toward idolatry be. The prophets of Baal can be characterized as simply a professional ministry trained in gratifying the felt-needs of the masses clamoring for their own preeminence. And its proponents may believe just as strongly in the miraculous power of their popular religion as the prophets of Baal did. But as important as determining the nature and extent of idolatry today, an even more pertinent question may be gleaned from the story of Elijah. Not discovering its extent or form, but rather establishing the proper response to idolatry in all its forms and extent. It is obvious that we cannot take such drastic measures as the prophet Elijah, but can we afford not to take our own quest for preeminence seriously, and still claim to worship the God that this self-idolatry seeks to displace? Unless we confront our consumer giant of "me first," we will attempt to make everything (God, Bible, gospel) bow down to our idol of self.

So, in the face of idolatry, what are we to do? Where would the preacher take us? Can't we just pray a quick prayer and continue on our merry way? Or perhaps he will reaffirm that we are now in Christ, and our idolatries have already been forgiven past, present and future. Certainly, he cannot just leave us here, like the prophets of Baal, slain in the temple (figuratively speaking). Don't we deserve better? That depends on what's most important, ourselves or God. Our response to idolatry always reveals our love for God. This preacher was obviously of the opinion that the recognition of our idolatries was not the most terrible thing that can happen to us, but the first step in resolving the most terrible thing that has happened to us; and that gospel-comfort is not always the most valuable thing that we need from a sermon. The secondary issue of comfort would only be paramount to an audience who love themselves with all their heart, and therefore always focus on themselves first. And if we say that both our love to God and for ourselves are equally important, then we are not seeking to love God with all our hearts, but merely to divide our love equally between God and ourselves. Loving ourselves is a legitimate love, but only as a subordinate love; otherwise, it is idolatry. This idolatry is even more serious than simply choosing a lesser good over the supreme. It is exalting ourselves over God and is ultimately revealed in our choosing our own will over His. The fact that self-idolatry opposes the very nature of God, and not merely that this idolatry is against our own good, implies that no preacher can either minimize its seriousness, or too quickly comfort his hearers with "peace, peace," without revealing a love for God that is subordinate to the love he has for himself and man.

The Bible is consistent on this issue, and always has the same attitude towards idolatry. Are there any verses that flip the scales in our direction and assert that divided affections, while very undesirable, are somehow more permissible and less serious under grace? Does grace or gospel ignore the heart, or do they change it? Although some verses can be twisted to infer the former by indirect implication, one direct declaration can never be contradicted by a hundred indirect implications. What is not clear can never contradict that which is clear. "Thou shall love the Lord thy God with all thine heart, soul, mind and strength," is never replaced by the gospel of "Let us love ourselves with all our heart." When James warns of spiritual adultery, and John of losing our first love or being lukewarm, and Paul of the dangers of legalism or being carnal, it is always communicated with the utmost seriousness and call for change. There is no indication that those who were the direct recipients of these warning had the option to view them as anything but serious. The indirect implication of only confessing our failure and trusting in God's grace alone for forgiveness is incompatible with the seriousness of the problems, unless the direct call to change our ways is also heeded. There is no biblical quick fix that solves the problems that concern us, while ignoring God's preeminent concern for His own glory. So, in the light of the gospel, the real indirect implication of all these verses is not that we are imperfect and therefore excused, but that we are imperfect and empowered, and therefore are called upon to make the appropriate change. Discipleship is a call to follow Christ, and not an indirect call to humbly accept our inability to follow.

When Peter repeats the Old Testament command, "Be ye Holy; for I am holy," does the force of his appeal now change in the New Testament? Is this direct declaration ever contradicted anywhere in the Bible? Or did Paul qualify it because now "the good pleasure of His will" is "to exalt the praise of the glory of His grace, wherein He hath made us accepted in the Beloved?"[1] God's grace is always unmerited, but does His grace only encompass one single aspect salvation, or does it include the whole? Does it deliver us only from the guilt of our idolatries in justification, or does it also deliver us from the power of them in regeneration and sanctification? Whichever grace we choose to accept reflects our attitude toward idolatry and reveals our true love for God.

To fight the fundamentalist half-battle of the mind is not enough when the real battle is for the heart, soul, mind and strength. Theology that consoles its recipients in the practice of that which is an abomination to God does not recognize the seriousness of sin, because it does not take God seriously. The fact that some can believe something so strongly based on an indirect implication alone, leaves them without excuse for rejecting that which is clearly a direct declaration. Yes, the Corinthians acted carnally, but

---

[1] Ephesians 1:6.

where does the Bible directly declare that this is an acceptable or excusable state. Verses like these reflect a reality that needs to be taken seriously, not excused. In the Bible, words delivered for the purpose of encouraging change, should never be employed to discourage it, or render us comfortable without change. The fact that the Bible corrects much in the lives of believers, does not imply that change is optional but that it is a reasonable scriptural expectation. There is a reason why the Spirit inspired the Scriptures to be predominantly practical. And it was not because God is demanding, but because He is deserving. Iain Murray wrote,

> The Christian's character and godliness is given higher priority in Scripture than his service. Therefore all seeking of spiritual enjoyment or of public usefulness apart from personal holiness is delusive[2]

In view of God's mercies (everything from election to glorification), Paul beseeches the Roman believers to "present your bodies a living sacrifice, holy, acceptable unto God, which is your reasonable service."[3] For Paul, the practical side of his epistles were not add-ons, but equally vital parts of the message that he wanted to convey. The commands that follow Paul's call to reasonable worship are no less optional than the call to worship itself, for, once again, they were not given because God is demanding but deserving. They are not mere practical advice added on to the more essential doctrines of the faith that preceded. For Paul, inactivity and indifference were not the expected outcome of the of the message of the gospel. The word gospel occurs 104 times in the New Testament, and 10 of those times are in 1 Corinthians chapter nine, between verses 12 and 23. In verse 23 Paul writes,

> And this I do for the gospel's sake, that I might be partaker thereof with you.

And with the gospel clearly in his mind, he goes on to express the true gospel-centered response of the believer in the following verses,

---

[2] Iain H. Murray, *Pentecost – Today?* (Carlisle: The Banner of Truth Trust, 1998), 130.
[3] Romans 12:1.

Know ye not that they which run in a race run all, but one recieveth the prize? So run, that ye may obtain. And every man that striveth for the mastery is temperate in all things. Now they do it to obtain a corruptible crown; but we an incorruptible. I therefore so run, not as uncertainly; so fight I, not as one that beateth the air: But I keep under my body, and bring it into subjection: lest that by any means, when I have preached to others, I myself should be a castaway.

In the context of 1 Corinthians 9, the "preaching to others" refers back to the gospel. True gospel-centeredness teaches that we must now do our all for Christ's glory precisely because He has done all for us. If both sides (theological and practical) are equally conducive to the glory and honor of God, then those who do not strongly endorse both sides must, one way or another, oppose God's glory. Gospel-centered idolatry, then, that focuses primarily on one side or the other (legalism or antinomianism), opposes the very glory of God. It is a bad sign when we pray like the Pharisee, "I thank God I am not like this sinner." But it is equally alarming when we pray as sinners, "I thank God I am not like this Pharisee." For the publican in the parable was not looking around at anyone but himself and God.

If our goal is to reach an audience of idolaters, then our preaching will attempt to render the message more relevant and less offensive to an audience who focuses only on themselves first, or it will seek to attract with the offer of lesser things, whether in the life or the next. Included in these lesser things are those that are relatively good and outwardly moral. But they are counterfeits, nonetheless, if they only serve to strengthen our self-centeredness. The gospel itself is a most excellent thing, but if it is employed to reinforce our self-centeredness, rather than call us from it, then it is a counterfeit gospel. Therefore, the Bible speaks of the danger of "another Jesus," "another spirit" and "another gospel"[4] that threaten the church.

Based on the worship/idolatry test, the Bible is self-authenticating. It is not man trying to reach God for the advantages to be gained or the dangers to be avoided alone. Although the Bible does not delegitimize any of these secondary motives, but rather encourages them, it also supersedes them with

---

[4] 2 Corinthians 11:4.

a motivation infinitely higher than ourselves. Thus, Christianity frees us not in a negative direction to forget about ourselves and all the good things God has created, but in a positive direction to value God infinitely above ourselves and anything else. This love for God that is lacking in me-centered worship is not gained by simply reflecting on all the wonderful things that God has done for us in Christ. It loves God because it has tasted the loveliness of His nature reflecting from His word in regeneration and seeks to increase in that knowledge in sanctification.[5] "The love of God is shed abroad in our hearts by the Holy Ghost which is given unto us."[6] Initially it is a passively received, for "when we were enemies, we were reconciled to God by the death of His Son."[7] But the gospel does not end here, for the verse continues, "much more, being reconciled, we shall be saved by His life." The immediate benefits of the gospel are passively received (justification and regeneration), but the further benefits are actively received as the believer strives, fights, runs, watches and prays in the power of the Spirit.

This raises an important question that must be answered directly and clearly. How do we apply the test of reasonable worship to our preaching, our theology or even our own lives, since we are all so weak and imperfect? Karl Barth is an example of imperfection. Although considered one of the greatest theologians of the 20th century by many, he continued to have a mistress along with his marriage. But the test of whether he is merely an imperfect disciple, like the rest of us, or no disciple at all, was not that he fell, nor how often he fell, but that he theologically justified his right to continue falling, rather than obey God. So, the test of a gospel-centered idol worshiper is not necessarily whether one falls into sin, nor how often he falls, but rather one's attitude towards his fall. The test of idolatry in both the Old and New Covenants begins with an attempt to rationally declare God unworthy of worship by removing or lessening the imperative from the command in our theology or preaching. Our attempts may appear pious and even Christ-centered, "I are eternally secure in Christ, whether I obey or not." It is true that our security is in Christ and not our obedience, but we do not obey to merit our future salvation, but because our hearts have been changed and Christ now

---

[5] John 17:17; 2 Peter 3:18.

[6] Romans 5:5.

[7] Romans 5:10.

commands our affections and deserves obedience. So, the "whether or not" verbiage comes from the heart of an idolater. Paul would answer such a hypothetical assertion with "God forbid." It is God's glorious excellencies that render optional obedience no longer a reasonable part of the believer's vocabulary of worship. The very fact that we are alright with lowering the force of the commands simply because the personal consequences have been dealt with, proves that Christ does not have our affections and our self-idolatry remains. This self-idolatry is exposed by inventing a theology that transforms Christ's work into an idol that we utilize to maintain the legitimacy of our option not to obey. While no child of God obeys perfectly, if we invent a theology that allows us to take sin less seriously, then an exaggerated love for the idol of self has blinded us to the glory of God. For the gospel clearly affirms that the reason man deserves wrath is because God deserves worship. They both rise and fall together. Once the gospel is freely received by faith alone, through grace alone, the believer is not to attempt to change the message to infer that now that man no longer gets what he deserves (wrath), he no longer has to be too concerned whether God gets what He deserves (worship).

Self-idolatry can hide in both Calvinism and Arminianism in the form of either antinomianism or legalism. Thus, we can employ our very theology to condone our idolatry. Justification and sanctification are two separate benefits of salvation. In justification, God declares that He is for us. In sanctification we declare with our lives that we are for Him. The former takes place in God, while the latter takes place in us. One is past tense and continues the same forever, for God never changes. The other, although it began in the past, should always be progressing, for its consummation is yet future. Sanctification, should always be viewed experimentally. The tree is known by its fruit. To ascertain to genuineness of our worship, we must examine both our lives and our theology to see whether they oppose or promote true worship before we claim the title of worshiper. We are not looking for perfection, but direction. If one benefit of Christ's gospel excludes another in our theology, then it will constantly point us in the wrong direction.

Let us assume that we are among those whom God has already declared righteous. Although gratitude for this blessing will affect our present walk, what does that walk itself look like? How does the gospel save us? True gratitude is not always attempting to squeeze out of the gospel more and more of our preferred consumer benefits to meet our felt-needs. The tone of gratitude is both triumphant and militant. The Arminian believes that only those who persevere to the end will be saved. This is militant but not triumphant. The Calvinist believes that all who are truly saved will persevere onto the end. This is triumphant and militant. But many modern Christian believes that God will preserve them, whether they persevere in faith and holiness or not. This is triumphant but not militant. It implies at least the possibility that the gospel can save us from God's wrath, but not from ourselves. This makes reasonable worship, which includes the continuous acts of faith and repentance, optional, simply because we have already performed a single act of faith in the past.

Nor are we to merely remember our deliverance from wrath and hell only to fulfill some psychological need of the present. Moses told the children of Israel, "beware lest thou forget the Lord, which brought thee forth out of the land of Egypt, from the house of bondage"[8] not so they would feel safe and secure in the hands of such a mighty God, but so that they would not go back again into bondage. The whole book of Deuteronomy is forward looking. "He brought us out from thence, that He might bring us in."[9] The deep consideration of all God's mercies is to move us forward. The rear-view mirror serves no purpose, if the car has no intension of moving forward. In this way, we use our rear-view theology to impede our walk. This the Bible never does. Whether in the prophets or the epistles, the Bible is always pointing people forward; always correcting some deficiency; always calling us on to perfection. Hebrews is a very theological book, but the main purpose of the book was to encourage perseverance. Even in Philippians, where Paul is addressing no compelling problem, this forward-looking call rings out most eminently. Paul writes,

> Nor as though I had already attained, either were already perfect: but I follow after, if that I may apprehend that for which also I am apprehended of Christ Jesus. Brethren, I count not myself to have apprehended but this one thing I do, forgetting those things which are behind, and reaching forth unto those things which are

---

[8] Deuteronomy 6:12.
[9] Deuteronomy 6:23.

before, I press toward the mark for the prize of the high
calling of God in Christ Jesus.[10]

Although looking back has its proper place, a looking-back Christianity
alone is only an option for those professors who still worship themselves.
It refuses to acknowledge a God worthy of a race, a fight or a pilgrimage.
Our very theology can oppose worship, when it implies that: "the battle is
over"; "Christ has already won"; "we are only to wait for the Christ who we
love to come to us, (and, in the meantime, save as many souls as we can)."
While these statements may be true when referring to Christ's work on
our behalf in justification, they deny the multifaceted work of Christ that
also extends to our lives in regeneration and sanctification. Paul describes
both the call and the walk together when writing to the Thessalonians,

> That ye would walk worthy of God, who hath called you
> unto His kingdom and glory.[11]

> That our God would count you worthy of this calling,
> and fulfill all the good pleasure of His goodness, and the
> work of faith with power.[12]

For the calling of the gospel to be effectual it must be unto something
greater than ourselves. The walk that accompanies it should be with
power. When God counts us worthy, we walk worthy of God. Gospel-
centered idolatry succeeds in making Christianity something worthy of
man (useful, motivational, inspirational), but it also succeeds in making
it something unworthy of God. If the believer's obedience is not to earn
salvation, but to express worship, then those who seek to comfort any
with the option of little or no obedience, count God less worthy than the
idol of self that they seek to prop up in their lives. They may challenge
some to get serious in regard to future rewards, and this is a legitimate
concern, but the consideration of God's glorious nature alone will never
be a reasonable call to worship for those who focus only on themselves. It

---

[10] Philippians 3:12-14.
[11] 1 Thessalonians 1:12.
[12] 2 Thessalonians 1:11.

is not falling short of reasonable worship that discovers this idolatry. For while it is agreed that we all fall short, it is the tendency to theologically justifying this failure that reveals our self-idolatry. And gospel-centered idolatry removes the seriousness of idolatry by accustoming men to a gospel that maintains its primary usefulness by referring man back to their former identity as idolaters. Paul describes the former condition of all believers, when he writes,

> Who were dead in trespasses and sins; wherein in times past ye walked according to the course of this world, according to the prince of the power of the air, the spirit that now worketh in the children of disobedience: Among whom also we all had our conversation in times past in the lusts of our flesh and of the mind; and were by nature the children of wrath, even as others.[13]

Then he goes on to describe the present condition and walk of all who believe,

> Even when we were dead in sins, hath quickened us together with Christ, (by grace ye are saved;) And hath raised us up together . . . For by grace are ye saved through faith; and that not of yourselves: it is the gift of God: not of works, lest any man should boast. For we are his workmanship, created in Christ Jesus unto good works, which God hath before ordained that we should walk in them.[14]

The present condition of all believers includes both positional justification and experimental sanctification, among others. Justification is not all that is offered in the gospel and it is does not describe all that has occurred in the believer. Spiritual life has been imparted. They are born of the Spirit. They have become partakers of the Divine nature. So, when we identify believers primarily by what they were before conversion and apply

---

[13] Ephesians 2:1-3.
[14] Ephesians 2:5-10.

the gospel to them in the same way we would apply it to the lost sinner, we deny the power of the gospel to save. Does the gospel ever tell the sinner to "put off" or "put on" like it tells the saints? The believer cannot be justified again, for he has already received the sin-bearing Redeemer. Nor can he be pressed with the necessity of the new birth, for he has already received the regenerating Spirit. The call of the gospel for the believer is a call to worship for mercies received, and therefore cannot call him from that worship that is expressed in progressive sanctification. Since the sanctification of believers is not perfect, the believer must still draw near to Christ in confession and forsaking of sin for forgiveness, but all of these are included within the Spirit's present application of salvation in the life of the believer in sanctification and not his already perfect righteousness of justification. Sanctification take the problem of idolatry seriously, and its place in our theology and life show our attitude towards idolatry.

The deliverance that we seek to apply always reveals our worship, or lack thereof. Let's say we have all ascertained correctly the extent of our disease. The cure that we go on to recommend, then, will equally reveal what is important to us. If our theology declares that the glory of God is advanced simply by covering the symptoms with forgiveness, then we do not care to be cured of the self-idolatry that opposes God's glory, simply because the danger of God's wrath that threatened the idol of self has subsided. This proves that we have no concept of the glory of God nor the seriousness of the disease beyond its personal consequences to self. Biblical theology does not teach that our disease is eradicated, but neither does it point to a partial cure that renders us comfortable with it. The Spirit always opposes the flesh and cannot comfort us while we are not opposing it. We may derive comfort from the fact that our cancerous disease is not fatal, but the doctor who believes he needs only render us more comfortable with this non-life-threatening disease, while it continues to eat away at our flesh, does not take our disease seriously. We invent a theology that informs us that our disease must remain to keep us continually dependent on God, and then proceed to depend on Him for a partial deliverance that renders the disease not only less serious, but possibly even beneficial. "There is therefore now no condemnation to them which are in Christ Jesus."[15] Since this condemnation is now eliminated,

---

[15] Romans 8:1.

the primary application of the gospel toward believers is not the forgiveness of sin, but the mortification of sin by the Spirit. "For as many as are led by the Spirit of God, they are the sons of God."[16] Our concept of gospel as applied to believers can never contradict the Word nor nullify the work of the Spirit. Believers are no longer dead in trespasses and sins. They are alive in the Spirit. Although he who is most holy may see himself as most sinful because he sees sin more clearly in himself, when we begin to glory in who is the most conscious of his sinfulness only to show who is the most grateful for God's forgiving grace offered in the gospel, then we do not see sin clearly for what it is against God, but only in relation to ourselves. In this way, the idol factory of our soul can succeed in turning even Christ and grace into idols that promote what man desires above all else – a way to continue his self-idolatry; "turning the grace of our God into lasciviousness," which is always connected with "denying the only Lord God, and our Lord Jesus Christ."[17] The goal of the ministry of the false prophets in Jeremiah's day corresponds with the goal of gospel-centered idolatry –"They have healed the hurts of the daughters of my people slightly, saying, Peace, peace; when there is no peace."[18] An indirect denial of Christ worthiness of worship by directly denying the seriousness of the primary means to worship – obedience.

Our trust in the faithfulness of God, and our dependence upon Him, extends to all aspects of salvation. We are not only justified by faith, we are also sanctified by faith and walk by faith. The promises of God's faithfulness extend to both our standing and our walking. "God is faithful," yes, but continue reading the two-fold manifestation of His faithfulness,

> who will not suffer you to be tempted above that ye are able; but will with the temptation also make a way of escape, that ye may be able to bear it.[19]

"Faithful is He that calleth you, who also will do it," of course, but what is it that He is faithful to do?

---

[16] Romans 8:14.
[17] Jude 4.
[18] Jeremiah 8:11.
[19] 1 Corinthians 10:13.

And the very God of peace sanctify you wholly; and I pray
God your whole spirit and soul and body be preserves
blameless unto the coming of our Lord Jesus Christ.[20]

If we invent a theology that insists that God be faithful only to His
promises regarding justification and not to those promises regarding our
walk, we trust God's faithfulness only half way, and therefore deny His
faithfulness altogether. The power available in Christ is not a power in
which we do nothing, but a power without which we can do nothing. It is
a power directed toward activity, not inactivity. Even the call of the gospel
includes the commands to both faith and repentance. Our inability to
do either does not exempt us from obedience, because the very power of
the gospel unto salvation grants both of these as gifts. Neither faith nor
repentance can exist without the corresponding activity. The power of the
gospel manifests not only for man, but in man.

If we look at how the word grace is used in the books of 1st and
2nd Corinthians, the books that address more ethical issues than any
other epistle, it becomes evident that the grace they needed was one
that practically manifests and powerfully enables. Even the many times
Paul uses the term gospel in these two epistles, it is mostly connected to
activities such as preaching, or effects such as regeneration. So, to view
the gospel correctly, we must envision the strength of God more than
the weakness of man revealed by the law. Paul did not excuse their moral
failure by simply offering a mere covering for them, or a positional grace
that says, "It's not what we do that counts, it's what He has done." Nowhere
does the Bible offer such a partial cure to believers, because God cannot
endorse idolatry, even in the least degree.

The biblical expectation of change is based on the presumption
that grace and the gospel are powerful and effective, not ineffective.
Therefore, the exhortation is always forgiveness and cleansing; confessing
and forsaking. For Paul, what we do does count, if it is a result of what
Christ has done. Christ's work encourages our work, because now the
"spiritual sacrifices" that we offer up are "acceptable to God by Jesus
Christ."[21] Such sacrifices are not only a consequence, but the very purpose

---

[20] 1 Thessalonians 5:23-24.
[21] 1 Peter 2:5.

xix

that we, "as lively stones, are built up a spiritual house, a holy priesthood, to offer up spiritual sacrifices." The fact that these sacrifices are only "acceptable to God by Jesus Christ," and are not meritorious nor perfect, does not eliminate them as the grand purpose for the church. Any view of either grace or gospel in the life of the believer that minimizes the necessity of good works, minimizes the power of both grace and the gospel; thereby, limiting Christ's sacrifice, and reducing His grand purpose for the church to merely relieving the consequences of our spiritual fall without remedying it. The fact that one can come to Christ and consider discipleship optional or of minimal importance shows that he has rejected the offer, power and loveliness of Christ and the gospel.

The problem with many of the writings that come out of the gospel-centered community is that their views of grace and the gospel are too one-sided and limited. It is good news that justification and adoption are direct benefits that result from the sacrifice of Christ on the cross. But if we truly love God, it is equally good news that regeneration and sanctification are also both direct benefits from Christ's death. In their zeal to exalt one side to the minimizing of the other, they accuse those of attempting to add to Christ's finished work, who are merely seeking to experience the direct benefit of that work by the Spirit. Although none of these writers fail to mention these other benefits, they are not equally esteemed. Therefore, they speak of a "transforming positional view"[22] In listing all the benefits of the cross in his book *Gospel Deeps*, Jared Wilson seems to forget to mention regeneration altogether. Referring to sanctification in the same list, he writes,

> The initial sanctification then and even the ongoing sanctification now are the effects of the cross-cause, the outworking of our justification.[23]

Making one benefit of Christ's death (justification) the producer of another (sanctification), is impossible without both turning justification into a work and rendering sanctification passive. Justification does not

---

[22] Jared C Wilson, *Gospel Deeps: Reveling in the Excellencies of Jesus* (Wheaton: Crossway, 2012), 47.
[23] Ibid, 98.

effect sanctification. It is the agency of the Spirit and the instrumentality of the Word that promote progressive sanctification. What is really being expressed is a salvation that is all one-sided. "The gospel's announcement of salvation is fundamentally salvation from the wrath of God,"[24] he writes. By centering the problem on God's side (wrath), the real problem of spiritually death and self-idolatry are now considered less serious. Therefore, he ends his book with a one-sided solution quoted from Tullian Tchividjian,

> Santification is the hard work of going back to the certainty of our already secured pardon in Christ and hitting the refresh button over and over.[25]

Another easy solution that ignores the real work of sanctification by covering it in forgiveness. Is going back to our already secured pardon really hard work or does false presumption come naturally? The problem here is that the reset button of positional truth cannot be reset over and over without becoming works righteousness. Comingling justification with sanctification does not enhance the doctrine of justification, as he supposes, it rather turns justification into a means to sanctification. And no matter how many times we press the reset button of pardon, this could never compete with those original multifaceted blessings of Christ's death conferred on the believer at conversion. It is the totality of these, and not any single one individually, that motivate sanctification according to Paul. The wrath we deserved was not resolved so that the worship that God deserves could be avoided. The reset button of pardon is never described as the means to sanctification, but a part of the ongoing work of sanctification; therefore, the believer's confession and forgiveness are not the maintenance or continuation of his justification.

Going back to the certainty of our already secured pardon does not even solve the problem of legalism. While no legalist is a believer, the believers may sometimes act legalistically, as though their deeds had merit toward either their ultimate salvation or future rewards. While even this sin does not eliminate their justification, the proper response is not to merely

---

[24] Ibid, 101.
[25] Ibid, 200.

remind them of their justification and encourage them to hit the refresh button and go on their merry way. This sin, like every other sin, must be confessed as an attack on Christ's preeminence, and repented of, or we will only hit the refresh button for the idol of self. In this way those who make sanctification merely getting used to our justification, invent a deliverance that doesn't take man's idolatry seriously. Gospel-centered sanctification, contrary to Spirit empowered sanctification, produces a false freedom by normalizing and necessitating a continual non-sanctification. True gospel sanctification does not redefine sanctification through the lens of justification. For, like oil and water, they are two different things that do not flow from one another and cannot be mixed.

This partial view of deliverance especially shows up in their writings that deal specifically with sanctification and discipleship. For example, in his book, *The Imperfect Disciple: Grace for the People Who Can't Get Their Act Together,* Jared C. Wilson applies the gospel to disciples when he writes,

> This is why the good news is so good! The essential message of Christianity isn't "do" but "done." The good news is news, not instruction, and it announces to us not "get to work" but "it is done."[26]

This statement is true as to the grounds of salvation, but false if we apply it to the fruit of salvation, which includes our discipleship. Paul describes salvation as both work and fruit in the life of the believer,

> Work out your own salvation with fear and trembling. For it is God which worketh in you both to will and to do of His good pleasure.[27]

The message for believers, everywhere throughout the epistles is "work" and "do." The fact that there are no perfect disciples cannot be disputed, because following is all about direction, not perfection. But one benefit of Christ's death (justification) cannot eliminate or minimize

---

[26] Jared C. Wilson, *The Imperfect Disciple: Grace for People Who Can't Get Their Act Together* (Grand Rapids: Baker Books, 2017), 67.
[27] Philippians 2:12,13.

another (sanctification). And discipleship is included in the latter, not the former. If we invent a theology that allows us to take less seriously the call to present our bodies a living sacrifice, all because of Christ's ultimate sacrifice, then we accept a theology that uses the motive to worship (God's mercies) as a means to covertly redefine worship. The teaching that minimizes submission to the Lordship of Christ, which is the essence of discipleship, does not cherish the preeminence of Christ, because it makes that which exalts the preeminence of Christ optional. Since worship cannot be directly ignored in Christianity, it's essence must be redefined. "But isn't Christ glorified in all that He has done for us, that no one should boast?" we quickly object. Yes, but the call to discipleship is not a reaffirmation of Christ's loyalty to ourselves, it calls us to loyalty to Him. It is true that salvation is solely by grace through faith in Christ and the gospel, but Mark tells us that our esteem for both Christ and the gospel, or the test of being both Christ-centered and gospel-centered, are reflected in a life of discipleship:

> Whosoever will come after Me, let him deny himself,
> and take up his cross, and follow Me. For whosoever
> will save his life shall lose it; but whosoever shall lose his
> life for My sake and the gospel's, the same shall save it.

"For My sake and the gospel's" shows the real motivation for discipleship, and if we minimize discipleship, it is an evidence of wrong motives. If works are not done to merit, but to express salvation, then we cannot pit Christ's saving benefits one against another. Satan knows that he must cover his counterfeits under right sounding phrases, such as gospel-centered discipleship; therefore, Jared Wilson employs a looking-back solution to a forward-looking endeavor, which result is self-love, rather than self-denial. He writes,

> But what I really need is to rehearse what he's already
> done for me, what he's already done in Christ that
> satisfied my desires, met my needs, and answered my

longing. In the rush to emotional outburst, I miss affectionate rememberings.[28]

Here, claiming to be gospel-centered, he turns discipleship totally upon its head. Surely such one-sided rememberings produce me-centered obedience. He expresses this me-centered obedience when he writes,

> This relationship, born of the gospel, helps us see that His commands come from a place of love and are positioned for our good.[29]

While this may be true, it is still only one-sided. And, if we view things from God's perspective, it is the lesser of the two sides. Loving ourselves is a legitimate motive to obedience, if subordinate to loving God, for without a supreme love for God the only remorse that we would have towards sin would be for its negative affect on ourselves, and the focus of our obedience would be primarily on ourselves. Loving God only because he loves and blesses us does not take self-idolatry seriously, because it does not exalt God supreme in our affections, but only renders Him serviceable to self. If idolatry usurps God's rightful place in our affections, then the way we deal with it, or fail to deal with it, reveals our love for God. If "grace for people who can't get their act together" refers only to grace in the abstract, then the grace that comforts by ignoring the problem is all that is being is offered.

Taking from Paul's metaphor of "jars of clay," Jared describes those whom he apparently believes are imperfect disciples,

> We are fragile, and when we are broken what's inside is revealed. What we worship shows through. Every time we take a hit, our true self comes out. We can try to hide it in times of comfort and ease, but we can't keep our true self covered. The jar will crack. The fig leaves will rot and fall. Your true, rotten self will come out. But here's the good news. That real you, the you inside that you hide, the you that you try to protect,

---

[28] Ibid, 76.
[29] Ibid, 78.

the you that you hope nobody sees or knows – that's the you God loves. No, he doesn't love your sin, of course. But he loves your true self. Without pretense, without façade, without image management, without the religious makeup. You the sinner, you the idolater, you the worshiper of false gods – that's the you Jesus loves. Look, this is the whole point of the Christian message: God loves sinners.[30]

God loves sinners, true, but whether this is the whole point of the Christian message or even the main point should not be debated in a book dealing with discipleship that should insist on Christ's right to preeminence above all else. In discipleship we deny ourselves. Christ's mission is not to accept our true self but transform it. The flesh remains in believers, but we are to crucify it rather than accept it. God does not love it, nor should we accept it. If our response to idolatry always reveals our love for God, and the "you Jesus Loves" is "you the idolater," or "you the worshiper of false god's," as Wilson contends, then Christ's response to idolatry would prove that He did not love God. The goal of ministry would no longer be for Christ to be formed in us, but to show that Christ likes us just the way we are. This is a positional view of the gospel that is good news for the so-called disciple who doesn't take God serious enough to merit all our heart, soul, mind and strength. It is a call to affirm rather than deny ourselves.

Ironically, when it comes to the proper way to view ourselves, the author encourages his readers to take their positional truth in Christ very seriously. He writes,

> "I am not who they say I am; I am who God says I am,
> and I don't have to be an Osteen fanboy to say that and
> think that. I just have to be a Christian."[31]

Here, positional truth is used to promote self-idolatry, for when Osteen says these things, he actually believes that the Bible is all about man. This bad theology does not only condone divided affections and serving

---

[30] Ibid, 188.
[31] Ibid, 194,195.

two masters, it has flipped the scales of worship entirely in our direction. Unreasonable worship is the only viable alternative for those who accept a me-centered theology; therefore, they must seek to demonstrate theologically that the worship that Paul calls reasonable is nonexistent. Thus, the goal is not to humble man with a more glorious view of God, but to lower God to the centrality of man, and all under the guise of being gospel-centered.

In his book *The Gospel is for Christians*, Mitchell Chase gives "two reasons why beleivers need the gospel every day." In the second reason (we'll discuss the first reason later) he states,

> We need the gospel every day because, as justified sinners still living in a fallen world, we are prone to forget God rather than remember Him.[32]

The call to remember what God has done is needful, but if it is only a partial remembering, then it could reveal our gospel-centered idolatry. We must remember all the mercies received in the gospel to be truly grateful. When Paul writes about how God "hath blessed us with all spiritual blessings in the heavenly places in Christ,"[33] he goes on to include adoption, acceptance, forgiveness and redemption, but he begins with past election and ends with future glorification. And then, before he begins his long prayer for the Ephesian believers, he mentions the sealing of the Spirit as the immediate effect of believing the gospel. Paul never presents any one benefit as the whole gospel but includes them all from beginning to end, past, present and future. He writes the Roman Christian with a more comprehensive view of salvation,

> And we know that all things work together for good to them that love God, to them who love God, to them who are called according to His purpose. For whom He did foreknow, He also did predestinate to be conformed to the image of His Son, that He might be

---

[32] Mitchell Chase, *The Gospel is for Christians* (Brenham, TX, Lucid Books, 2010), 118.

[33] Ephesians 1:3-14.

the firstborn among many brethren. Moreover, whom He did predestinate, them He also called: and whom He called, them He also justified: and whom He justified, them He also glorified.[34]

Paul then included the promise of perseverance to this list at the end of the chapter.[35] All of these blessings are grounds for rejoicing. To exalt one above the others is to lower the one we are attempting to exalt, for the one becomes meaningless without the others. Even in Galatians, Paul insists on justification by faith as strongly as he insists on sanctification by the Spirit. At no time do the writers of the New Testament lower one benefit to give supremacy to another, for the supremacy belongs to Christ. And the real goal of eliminating all boasting is achieved not with gospel-centeredness (concern for the benefits alone), but Christ-centeredness (concern for the Bestower of benefits). Therefore, discipleship can be described as a life that cherishes the preeminence of Christ, because the only way to cherish His preeminence without boasting is to receive Him along with all His benefits (Christ-centeredness). For Christ to be all in all in our lives, we cannot view Him partially through one grace alone without attempting to hide ourselves from the full radiance of His glory.

> "That no flesh should glory in His presence. But of Him are ye in Christ Jesus, who of God is made unto us wisdom, and righteousness, and sanctification, and redemption: that according as it is written, He that glorieth, let him glory in the Lord."[36]

The view of Christ that glories in Him alone, receives all these things from Him. Herein lies the blindness to Christ's glory in the gospel-centered movement – they are trying to solve both a legal and a medical problem in a court of law, when they are two entirely different issues. If our spiritual condition is that we "are lovers of ourselves more than lovers of God," then, if God is the Judge, we have a legal problem that demands an Advocate,

---

[34] Romans 8:28-30.

[35] Romans 8:35-39.

[36] 1 Corinthians 1:29-31.

but we are also spiritually dead and need a Physician. If we invent a partial theology that only declares us righteous, then we will inevitably transform the essence of worship to accommodate this theology as the he only way God can receive the worship that He is due. "But we boast in this way," Wilson argues, "by owning up to how great a sinner we are because it is the only way to boast in the greatness of our Savior."[37] This very theology necessitates the continuation of the disease – our self-idolatry. Hence, from his man-centered view, unreasonable worship is now acceptable and expected. Victory is declared simply because the danger of our idolatry is removed, even if the personal affront to God remains. The fact that I am loyal only to myself poses no problem, because I have a great Savior who is just as loyal to me. According to this view, the life that cherishes the preeminence of Christ is no longer the life of discipleship, but the life that recognizes its non-discipleship. This is a gospel-centeredness that is limited to only one aspect of the gospel's power unto salvation. It implies that the only way to boast in the Savior who saved us, is to deny the Savior who continues to save us. This theology is man-centered rather than Christ-centered, because it only values the Savior for certain preferred benefits, thereby limiting His preeminence only to the preeminent concerns of man.

He ends his book by simply stating, "You are a great sinner, yes. But you have a great Savior."[38] The first question that comes to mind, in the context of discipleship which he writes, is whether we must remain a great sinner for Christ to remain a great Savior. "Shall we continue in sin, that grace may abound?"[39] Legitimate question when considering Paul's teaching on grace and justification. But Paul dealt with this objection with an immediate "God Forbid." And the immediate denial that Paul gives to the possibility of continuing in sin is not based on justification, but union with Christ. Free justification of the sinner raises this question, but the saint's union with Christ shows the answer. It is not surprising that we come up with a false solution, when we look for the answer in the wrong place. The how-two of sanctification is not found in justification, for justification solves a problem outside the realm of sanctification.

Gospel-centered idolatry does not refer to the saints as sinners to

---

[37] Ibid, 225.

[38] Ibid, 230.

[39] Romans 6:1.

keep them from being active in justification, but to render them passive in sanctification. It is used to deliberately ignore the problem. Referring to the first of two reasons why believers need the gospel every day, Mitchell Chase write, "First, believers are still sinners."[40] He is correct to say that the gospel is for believers, but wrong in how it applies to believers. He is not saying that believes still sin, for this would direct our attention to another benefit of the gospel – sanctification. He is saying that we are all still sinners, and in that context, we need the gospel. If he had said that we still need the gospel because we still sin, it would be clearly understood that he was referring to sanctification. But because he is referring to the gospel directed to the lost, he identifies the saints as sinners to direct them back to what every sinner needs - justification. But the gospel identifies the saints "in Christ." Look how Paul applied the gospel to himself:

> But if, while we seek to be justified by Christ, we ourselves also are found sinners, is therefore Christ the minister of sin? God forbid. For if I build again the things which I destroyed, I make myself a transgressor. For I through the law am dead to the law, that I might live unto God. I am crucified with Christ: nevertheless I live; yet not I, but Christ liveth in me: and the life which I now live in the flesh I live by the faith of the Son of God, who loved me and gave Himself for me.[41]

For Paul, the gospel application to himself was more personal, "who loved me and gave Himself for me." And this personal and vital union with Christ manifests in his life.[42]

Martin Luther's famous phrase "*simul iustus et peccator,*" simultaneously righteous and sinful, appears only once in his writings from his commentary on Galatians 3:6. The gospel does not call the sinner to act righteously (this is the message of the law), but it does call upon him to recognize that he has never acted righteously and can only be saved by a righteousness that is not his own. This righteousness is granted by grace alone through faith alone, while he is still in a sinful state. And no subsequent act

---

[40] Ibid, 116.
[41] Galatians 2:17-20.
[42] Read all of Romans chapter 6.

of righteous can ever add to nor take away from his justification. The righteousness wherein we are justified is already perfect. While Luther was right in using this phrase to describe justification accurately, we are wrong when we use it to explain sanctification. By referring to believers by what they were (sinners) and pointing back to what they have already passively received by the gospel (justification), many suppose that gospel sanctification is likewise received in the same way. Since we are all still sinners, according to this reasoning, sanctification, if it takes place at all, would be the mysterious result of constantly looking back to justification, as if sanctification somehow flows effortlessly out of justification, rather than from our union with Christ and the work of the Spirit.

The word sinner is used in the epistles to refer to what we once were prior to conversion (while we were yet sinners) or is included with a call to change (cleanse your hands ye sinners). So, to use the word sinners to express something that believer are just to accept as their normal identity is unwarranted. When we use such a term as a badge of honor to prove our humility, unless we also acknowledge our need to repent, we only show our prideful rebellion. When Paul calls himself the chief of sinners, he goes on to cite those sins committed before his conversion. Since we are called upon to follow Christ in discipleship, and not Paul, even if it were true that at the end of his ministry he was still the greatest sinner, and the gospel had made no impact on his life, can we proceed to infer by indirect implication that we all must be great sinners, too? We should follow Paul, but only insofar as he followed Christ.[43] The Bible directly command believers to consider themselves dead to sin.[44] We reject this direct command by choosing to identify ourselves as sinners who are only acting according to their true self when they sin, thereby rendering sin is less culpable and serious.

Gospel-centered idolatry is not revealed by the fact that we sin, nor by how often we sin, but by our attempt to make sin less serious. In the light of sins contrariness to God, the very attempt to normalize sin, by labeling all the saints as great sinners, without also calling for great change, is a statement of self-idolatry. Gospel-centered idolatry is not made known by acknowledging that we are imperfect discipleship, nor how imperfect of a disciple we are, but by the fact that it is a theology invented to allow and necessitate our non-discipleship in order to render the Savior more boast-worthy. This counterfeit gospel-centrality is void of the preeminence of

---

[43] 1 Corinthians 11:1.

[44] Romans 6:11.

Christ. The very preaching of the message of Christ may distract from Him, when we make the gospel all about us. The gospel becomes a call to an idol that we perceive as beautiful only because it promises to save, keep, protect and prosper our real idol – self. When our self-idolatry attracts us to Christianity, we have a deficient love for the Savior that is reflected in our partial views of deliverance. Whether this is accomplished under the guise of being gospel-centered, or under the boastful profession of works-righteousness, man's preeminence in his religion is secured, and the idolatry that is promoted by this theology will be revealed in preaching that attracts by legitimizing man's quest for his own preeminence. Theology that is based on a more glorious view of Christ will both call and deliver men from idolatry in all its forms and extent.

The preeminence of Christ will never be properly cherished in the heart so long as man remains the focus and Christ is valued primarily for His saving benefits to man. True Christianity is birthed in the heart by the Spirit who does nothing but what glorifies Christ. The goal of preaching, then, is not merely to explain how one can be blessed, but to ensure that these blessings reflect God's glory in both their essence, as well as in the way they are communicated; otherwise, such preaching will contradict the Father's design, devalue the Son's sacrifice and eliminate the need for the Spirit's application of salvation.

Those who see no beauty in Christ outside of how one can be benefited have lost the essence. The preeminence of Christ will not be cherished by those who desire the by-products of faith over its Object. For if all ends with us, it is a sign that we have no sight of the beauty, honor or glory of Christ.

Those who do not receive Him as a Prophet to guide, a King to rule and a Priest to make full atonement for sin, receive Him unworthily, and have lost the manner. To reject the words of the great Prophet who was to come, to refuse submission to the King of Kings, or to seek to be saved in some way other than by the great High Priest, is to receive Him in an unworthy manner, and so to overlook Him altogether. Faith not only appropriates Christ's work on our behalf, but also receives His person. It is not enough to believe that Christ is a prophet, priest and king, we must receive Him as our Prophet, Priest and King, thereby renouncing our wisdom, self-righteousness and quest for autonomy. Soteriology separated from a correct Christology, while correctly insisting on salvation by faith alone, will inevitable confuse the true nature of saving faith, and so rest in the mere faith of devils.

The gospel is powerful to save only insofar as it correctly communicates the Object of faith; not as all surpassing glorious because He is mighty to save, but mighty to save because He is all surpassing glorious. The difference can be subtle, but the end of all God's works, especially those wrought upon the soul, is His own glory. Since both the legalist and the antinomian oppose this glory by rendering glory to either the ability or preferences of the creature over and above the power and designs of the Creator, they are both excluded from this work. Neither require a supernatural work of God on the soul. Rather, they are both counterfeit offers that are packaged in such a way that allows one to embrace Christianity with either his self-righteousness or self-indulgence fully intact. To enable man to rest content with God's decretive will, and to gladly follow His perceptive will, man must be introduced by the Spirit into a life that cherishes the preeminence of Christ above his own personal preferences.

If discipleship is the life that cherishes the preeminence of Christ, then being consumer-driven promotes the life that despises the preeminence of Christ. We need a larger view of God that will eclipse our exaggerated view of ourselves before we can cherish the preeminence of Christ above the counterfeit offers of a consumer-driven Christianity that appeal to self. What the Puritans recognized was not merely that the gloriousness of Christ demands a total change of the whole of life, but that this change can only flow from a heart that has been changed by this glorious vision. Unlike the Pharisees, who embraced religion out of an elevated view of themselves and all that they could accomplish for God (or rather for themselves), the true disciple cherishes the preeminence of Christ above anything else that he hopes to gain by Him. What is it that draws you to Christ? The answer to this question is the difference between a true and a false professor. The apostle Peter demonstrates this contrast,

> Unto you therefore which believe He is precious: but unto them which be disobedient, the stone which the builders disallowed, the same is made the head of the corner, and a stone of stumbling, and a rock of offence, even to them which stumble at the word, being disobedient.[45]

---

[45] 1 Peter 2:7,8.

The cost of discipleship, then, is daunting only to those who have lost sight of the value of the treasure in the field. No price is too great for those who recognize its infinite worth. Those who make discipleship optional, minimize its cost or reject its terms, then, are blind to both the beauty and glory of Christ, and are forced to modify religion into that which promotes man's quest for his own supremacy.

Depravity, deliverance and discipleship (or guilt, grace and gratitude) are the three vital parts that encompass the whole of man's salvation. We cannot change the order, nor choose the most desired parts and ignore the rest, without overthrowing the whole. When we attempt to enhance the gospel with anything other than Christ, we are calling men away from Christ. This is what makes consumer-driven Christianity so deadly – it exalts the preferences of man and despises the preeminence of Christ.

> "There are three main parts of salvation: 1st, a true knowledge of our misery; 2nd, knowledge of our deliverance; and then a life conformable to the Word."[46]
>
> Richard Sibbes (1577-1635)

> "How many things are necessary for thee to know, that thou, enjoying this comfort, mayest live and die happy? Three; the first, how great my sins and miseries are; the second, how I may be delivered from all my sins and miseries; the third, how I shall express my gratitude to God for such deliverance."[47]
>
> The Heidelberg Catechism

The problem is not that man seeks his own happiness, but that he believes it does not lie down the path of this triple knowledge. He rather finds the counterfeit offers of a consumer-driven Christianity more appealing, and so chooses the path of self-indulgence over discipleship.

---

[46] Richard Sibbes, *Divine Meditations and Holy Contemplations* (London: J. Buckland, 1775), 82.

[47] *Heidelberg Catechism*, Question 2.

PART I

DEPRAVITY:

The Essence of the Consumer Nature

"Inasmuch as the measures which men employ for the promotion of religion will be chiefly determined by their conception of its nature, particularly of the natural state of man, and the state into which he must pass in order to become a child of God, and of that power and agency by which alone this change can be affected; it will facilitate our progress, to obtain a clear conception of those views of the nature of holiness, moral obligation, human depravity, regeneration, and repentance, which have formed the ground-work of these excitements."[48]

S. M. Woodbridge

---

[48] S. M. Woodbridge, *Princeton Review* Vol. 14 No. 1, 1842, 5.

CHAPTER 1

The Height of Duty, A Supreme Love for God

And behold, a certain lawyer stood up, and tempted Him, saying, Master, what shall I do to inherit eternal life? He said unto him, "What is written in the law? how readest thou?" And he answering said, "Thou shalt love the Lord thy God with all thy heart, with all thy soul, with all thy strength, and with all thy mind; and thy neighbour as thyself." And He said to him, "Thou hast answered rightly: this do, and thou shalt live." But he, willling to justify himself, said unto Jesus, "And who is my neighbour?"

Luke10:25 – 29

The first step in life's journey toward God is the recognition of our great distance from Him. For we can never descend appropriately into self-recognition without first ascending to the proper recognition of God. To understand the depths to which we have fallen, we must first understand the height from which we have fallen. While the brightness of His glory is revealed in the face of Christ Jesus, the extent of man's depravity is made known by the law. "I had not known sin, but by the law,"[49] said Paul. It is only in the light of His holy law, reflecting from His holy nature, that

---

[49] Romans 7:7.

1

the extent of man's duty is clearly revealed. This is the proper use of the law, which unless utilized, we cannot hope to be brought near unto God through Christ.[50]

All other rules will thwart our understanding of our divine obligation, producing a strictly man-centered morality that leaves man blind to the full extent of his depravity, while diminishing the seriousness of the requirements of God's law, and clouding His true nature in our eyes. Blind to the light of God's law and nature, man mistakes his prideful compassion toward others as true virtue, thereby never discovering the humbling reality of his deplorable condition in relation to God. It is only after we perceive the extent of our responsibility to God that we will accurately estimate the extent of our fall from Him.

But before we begin to explore the height of our duty to God, it is important to note that this discovery, while being the first and necessary step towards our recovery, does not necessarily effect it. The Jewish expert in the law, who came testing Jesus, knew the root of true religion in theory,[51] but this knowledge produced nothing more within him than the need to justify himself,[52] with no desire for change. The parable of the Good Samaritan that followed[53] revealed not only this lawyer's misapplication of his duty toward man, but also a total disregard for his highest duty toward God. By reserving the right to choose those more closely related to himself upon whom to exercise this universal duty, he clearly demonstrated that self was still at the center of his choice, for it was primarily the relationship of man to himself that determined his choice, not God. According to Christ, his love was no different from that of the pagans.[54] Despite all of his outward show, his depravity was in full force, because self was still his primary concern.

Our goal, then, is to discover the magnitude of the disease, so that we might affect an appropriate cure. And we can never discover the enormity of our disease by looking horizontally toward those who have likewise fallen with us into the depths of depravity. If we are to comprehend the

---

[50] Galatians 3:24.

[51] Luke 10:25 – 28.

[52] Luke 10:29.

[53] Luke 10:30 – 37.

[54] Mathew 5:46.

loftiness of the duty that we owe to God, and the great distance that we have fallen short of it, our eyes must first ascend to the height of God Himself. And once we comprehend the extent of our dreadful disease, we must continue to look vertically to God, and away from self or man, for an effectual cure. Only those who despair of their own strength and righteousness can hope to be candidates for this cure. "They that be whole need not a physician."[55]

Consumer-driven Christianity, by placing the height of man's duty no higher than the consumer is willing to ascend, strengthens man's depravity, rather than curing it. John Angell James counted this as "one of the prevailing defects of modern preaching" in his day. He clarifies,

> I mean the neglect of holding up this perfect mirror, in which the sinner shall see reflected his own moral image.[56]

Therefore, by closing its eyes to the extent and implications of God's law, consumer-driven Christianity also clouds the alluring brightness of His glory from its own eyes by exalting the exaggerated glory of defiled man. This limits the glorious extent and efficacy of Christ's work of recovering and transforming the human heart into a mere superficial morality and participation in outward religious activities.

Jeremiah Burroughs suggests, "The reason why people come and worship God in a slight way is because they do not see God in His glory."[57] Our understanding of the divine obligation is affected by an inadequate understanding of the divine nature. This inadequate understanding, and the ensuing moral consequences, can easily be seen in the rich ruler who also came asking Jesus the very same question as this lawyer:

---

[55] Matthew 9:12.

[56] Angell James, *An Earnest Ministry,* 83.

[57] Jeremiah Burroughs, *Gospel Worship* (Orlando: Soli Deo Gloria Publications, 1990; original, 1648).

"Good Master, what shall I do to inherit eternal life?
And Jesus said unto him, Why callest thou Me good?
None is good, save one, that is God."[58]

It would have served no purpose for Christ to reveal His deity to this ruler at this time, since his conception of deity was totally flawed. An accurate reflection on God's goodness always brings about the realization that there are none good, but God. A deep awareness of God's nature makes it impossible for one to freely attribute those perfections to mortal man, but will, by way of contrast, reveal man's imperfection. Whereas, the more readily we ascribe to men the different communicable attributes of God's nature, the more superficial our acquaintance must be with the real nature of both God and man. Because the extent of God's goodness and man's depravity are always seen in proportion to each another, we cannot have a higher view of the one, without a lower view of the other. Therefore, consumer-driven Christianity, by promoting only a superficial depravity that offends no one, equally endorses a superficial view of God that awes, inspires and ultimately saves no one.

Nor had this rich ruler come to truly understand the implications of God's commandments. Therefore, he could respond without the least hesitation, "All these have I kept from my youth up."[59] The greatest problem facing this rich ruler was not his depravity, but his blindness to his depravity. Men are apt to flatter themselves as better than they are, even in their vilest acts and under the most severe judgment of God over their lives.[60] And Consumer-driven Christianity, being another expression of this depraved tendency, further reinforces this blindness.

There is no personal interest to be gained by revealing to man the extent of his depravity, especially if we desire to attract the rich and powerful, but this is the path that we must follow if we are to prove our allegiance to the Father rather than the consumer. So, to prove his moral bankruptcy, Jesus said to him,

---

[58] Luke 18:18,19.
[59] Luke 18:21.
[60] Ezekiel 33:24 – 28.

> yet lackest thou one thing, sell all that thou hast, and
> distribute unto the poor, and thou shalt have treasure in
> heaven: and come, follow Me.[61] When he heard this, he
> was very sorrowful: for he was very rich.[62]

His sadness revealed that he had not even advanced past the first of God's commandments, "Thou shalt have no other gods before Me."[63] Nor the last of His commandment, "Thou shalt not covet."[64] He underestimated the extent of God's law, because he undervalued the perfections of God's nature reflected in the law. Never had the depths of his depravity been so unmistakably revealed, because the height of his duty had never been set so high. Like many, he had grasped, in theory, the necessity of a supreme love for God, but had never been challenged to demonstrate the reality of this love by renouncing the real object of his affection. Until then, he saw no evil in the secret idolatry of his own heart, which had been successfully hidden from the eyes of all but God. And it was not the degree of his descent into the baseness of degeneracy that revealed the depth of his depravity, but the failure to ascend to the height of a thorough recognition of the implications of a supreme love for God upon his own heart.

We, too, have reason for sadness the moment God ceases to be valued above whatever portion we have chosen above Him in our hearts, no matter how successfully we have been able to conceal this from others. Whether we are rich in wealth, rich in talent, rich in intellectual superiority, or rich in power, respect or outward morality, it is only the light of God's law and nature, rightly reflected upon, that reveals whether our allegiance is truly with God or something less. The more superficial our reflection upon God's law and nature becomes, the more ignorant we become, not only about God, but about ourselves. Therefore, like the rich ruler, we have chosen ourselves over the duty we owe to God, because we have chosen ourselves in the duty that we owe to Him, all the while imagining that we have somehow rendered to God His full due.

Duty is that which a person is bound to perform for others by any

---

[61] Luke 18:22.
[62] Like 18:23.
[63] Exodus 20:3.
[64] Exodus 20:17.

natural, moral or legal obligation, whether the inclination to do so or affection toward others exists in the heart. The essence of Christian duty, however, is altogether different. It does not rest in the outward performance alone but includes the inner inclination and affection toward God and others. "Owe no man anything, but to love one another: for he that loveth another hath fulfilled the law."[65] Love, which is the fulfillment of the law, is often presented as the solution to fulfilling God's commandments. But far from being the easy solution that we seek, it is this commandment to love that is the most difficult command of all. Our unawareness of its difficulty proves our ignorance of our depravity. It is more than the power of the will to act in a loving way, irrelevant of the intention of the heart. God requires that we have a heart that loves, for "the end of the commandment is charity out of a pure heart."[66] "Love one another with a pure heart."[67] A forced love is no love at all. How can we be commanded to love, then, when love can never be forced? Why are we commanded to do that which we are unwilling to do? Regeneration holds the key to the solution that we seek. What He requires of us is that we make ourselves a new heart, and not merely a new conduct. The prophet Ezekiel admonished, "Make you a new heart and a new spirit."[68]

The height of man's duty is a height beyond the reach of depraved man, because God requires more than a mere outer conformity to a list of rules. Therefore, God must implant a new affection within the heart. "The Lord thy God will circumcise thine heart......to love the Lord thy God with all thine heart, and with all thy soul."[69] This necessary change of heart not only secures the outer performance, it also implies the utter hypocrisy of all outer performances where this inner disposition is lacking. Performing merely out of a sense of duty alone is not enough. Thus, our duty is raised to include both the right action as well as a right heart that prompts the action. Gardinar Spring describes the relationship that exist between outer action and inner affection when he writes:

---

[65] Romans 13:8.
[66] 1 Timothy 1:5.
[67] 1 Peter 1:22.
[68] Ezekiel 18:31.
[69] Deuteronomy 30:6.

> Religious impulses, where they lead not to religious
> duties and active virtue, are just as spurious and joyless
> as the active virtue without the religious impulse.[70]

Thus, our duty rises above the cleaning of the outside of the cup to include the inside as well.[71] "Either make the tree good, and his fruit good; or else make the tree corrupt, and his fruit corrupt: for the tree is known by his fruit."[72] What determines the goodness of the actions of the body is the singleness of the eye with which it is performed – the motives and intentions of the heart.[73]

We will only recognize the degree of our depravity to the extent that we recognize what it means to "love the Lord thy God with all thy heart, and with all thy soul, and with all thy might."[74] The significance that we assign to this command will always correspond with the worth we ascribe to God Himself. Therefore, they are incapable of clearly perceiving the height of the duty that is due to such an exalted Being, to whom the worth of God has never been clearly revealed. The goal of evangelism, then, is not merely to show the dangers of hell and the glories of heaven, but the glories of God. Otherwise, men will only consider themselves and their own glory in religion. This renders true religion all the more impossible.

As the consciousness of God's worth rises in our estimation, so too will the height of the duty that we owe to Him equally ascend. If our goal in evangelism is to show the value and worth of the customer, by revealing only what Christ has done for him, then we will produce the opposite effect. Hence, the raise of all that Christ opposed in His earthly ministry: the centrality of man, the rise of celebrities within the church that compete with Christ's glory, and the embracing of religion merely for self-advantage.

The only reason that the depravity of our hearts is not so shockingly obvious, is because we hold God in so little esteem. Therefore, the command to love God with all our heart, soul, mind and strength is

---

[70] Gardinar Spring, *The Contrast between Good and Bad Men* (New York: M. W. Dodd, 1855), 323.

[71] Mathew 23:25 – 26.

[72] Mathew 12:33.

[73] Mathew 6:22 – 23.

[74] Deuteronomy 6:5.

quickly rushed over, while we love to linger on thoughts of His great love for us. His love for us is exceedingly great. And the reason is not because there is any greatness found in ourselves, but because He who is so infinitely worthy to be loved gave Himself for those who were so infinitely unworthy of that love. And the only just consideration of His great love for us should never terminate in self, but always reflect on His infinite worthiness by compelling a delightful compliance to the command to love Him with all our heart, soul, mind and strength. The only logical way to excuse ourselves from this duty is to first convince ourselves that God is no longer worthy of it, and not that we are no longer capable of it. And His unworthiness is what we preach to the world by proclaiming a feel-good gospel that either eliminates or lessens our obligation to God, no matter how incapable we are of its performance.

Our duty to love God with all our heart is a call to focus our supreme attention, thoughts and affections back on God, and away from self. When such supreme love exists in the heart, one would never desire to subordinate the supreme Object of his affection by refocusing his supreme love and attention back on himself. Thus, self-centered religion is a contradiction in terms. The work of Christ on the cross rebounds unto the glory of God. Therefore, it should never be employed in such a way that it strengthens our self-centeredness. For if true love for man "seeketh not her own,"[75] but rather gives of itself unselfishly in the service of others,[76] then certainly true love for God, who is the source of all true love for man, since we are "taught of God to love one another,"[77] cannot be self-seeking nor self-serving. A selfish love is no real love at all. True Christian freedom is freedom from the slavery of selfishness.[78] Counterfeit Christianity has always opposed this work of God on the soul by capitalizing on the selfish principle in man. Selfish man has always been willing and able to express self-centered love towards God ever since the fall. And he continually seeks to incorporate it into his religion in the form of a consumer-friendly Christianity; one that attracts man, because it is invented by man and for man.

---

[75] 1 Corinthians 13:5.

[76] Galatians 5:13.

[77] 1 Thessalonians 4:9.

[78] Galatians 5:13.

The fact that man's heart was turned from God to self in the fall, and that man no longer comes to God nor submits to His authority, but rather flees from Him, does not in any way lessen his obligation, nor excuse his failure to love God with all his heart, soul, mind and strength. For this obligation is universally imposed based on God's own worthiness, and not on what we have become, nor on whatever limitations we now possess. Therefore, God will not accept the plea of inability. The strength we lack, we are to go to Him to receive. If we are to climb to the height of our duty, we must seek a higher help. Such help man will not seek, not only because he is impotent, but primarily because he is obstinate. "There is none that seeketh after God,"[79] for there are none who desire Him. The will must first be turned before the man will turn. "God draws all His true people," said William Plumer, "but He will drag none to heaven contrary to their wills."[80]

Man's inability does not render secondary (or selfish) motivations necessary for the fulfillment of his primary obligation to love God with all his heart. For this obligation is imposed based on God's own worthiness to receive it, and not on whether man is benefited by it or not. Every desire after God that is inspired primarily by a desire to benefit self is a statement of the worthiness of self, and thus the unworthiness of God. For the more our motivations point to self, the less they point to God. Therefore, when the path of Christianity is determined by the preferences of the customer, it always leads away from God.

Self-love in God is not evil. When He loves Himself, He only loves that which is infinitely lovely, and should be loved supremely by all. But when man loves himself supremely, he loves that which is not only inferior, but, because of his depraved nature, opposite to all that is infinitely lovely, namely God. Therefore, inordinate self-love in man is infinitely evil, because it despises or competes with the loveliness of God. To the degree that we see the attractiveness of His holiness, we will recognize the comparative unattractiveness of our unholiness.

God's holiness consists in His love for Himself, and to that end He sanctifies Himself (sets Himself apart for this one purpose). Man's holiness

---

[79] Romans 3:11.

[80] William Plumer, *Vital Godliness: A Treatise on Experimental and Practical Piety* (New York: The American Tract Society, 1864), 42.

consists in his being set apart for that same purpose. When God bestows His love on man, He does so only in such a way that is consistent with His love for Himself. God's display of sacrificial love on the undeserving on the cross is a display of the highest kind of love; an expression of that eternal love that has always existed in God. Far from centering on man and inciting self-love, it reveals God's very essence, and is therefore the death of all misguided self-love. The soul permitted to see such love will find it so captivating that it must embrace it along with the duty that it entails, and so be drawn from its self-centered existence. To remain selfish is to not be drawn by Christ's self-sacrificing love at all, but to be drawn solely to the by-products of that love.

CHAPTER 2

The Height of Duty, The Believer's Delight

Wherefore, my beloved, as ye have always obeyed, not as in my presence only, but much more in my absence, work out your own salvation with fear and trembling. For it is God which worketh in you both to will and to do of His good pleasure.

Philippians 2:12,13

There is a big difference between loving that which is lovely for its own loveliness and loving it for the sake of its benefits. Although both exist in the child of God, the former is proof that we are true children of God, while solely possessing the latter is proof that we are not. It proves that we do not find God's eternal qualities so compelling that we sell all and lose all for Him. And the reason is not weak faith, but no faith at all. To the inquiry "Into the first and chief reason why the generality of Christians fall so far short of the holiness and devotion of Christianity," George Whitefield answers,

> because the generality of those who call themselves Christians are destitute of a true, living faith in Jesus Christ; for want of which they never effectually intended

to please God in all actions of life, as the happiest and best thing in the world.[81]

Faith must have an object. When God is revealed, there is no lovelier Object. Unless we have come to know Him as "altogether lovely,"[82] far lovelier than self, then we have not yet come to know Him at all. Charles Hodge explains,

> The perception of beauty is of necessity connected with the feeling of delight. Assent to moral truth involves the feeling of moral approbation. In like maner spiritual discernment (faith when the fruit of the Spirit) includes delight in the things of the Spirit, not only as true, but as beautiful and good. This is the difference between a living and a dead faith.[83]

Faith does not mean that believers escape duty. Faith makes it possible for him to "work out his own salvation." While we are not to trust in these works, neither are we to fear them. Such works, as the fruit of the Spirit, are to be fully expected, for if God works in us, it is always "both to will and to do of His good pleasure."[84] It is this willingness that turns duty into delight. And where this willingness is lacking, there can be no delight. Without delight, the performance is only pretense, and therefore not essentially the work that God accepts from nor performs upon the new creature. It is the new birth that changes duty into delight, and on this point, we are all agreed. But it does not, as some suppose, lessen our obligation to duty. How can duty be changed into delight, if it is eliminated?

Nor can God modify our duty towards Himself to conform with our desires, for our duty to love and obey any person always corresponds with the loveliness and authority of that person. Therefore, we are infinitely

---

[81] John Gillies, *Memoirs of Rev. George Whitefield* (Middletown: Hunt & CO., 1841), 642,643.

[82] Song of Solomon 5:16.

[83] Charles Hodge, *Systematic Theology, Vol. 1* (Grand Rapids: Eerdmans Publishing Company, reprint), 50.

[84] Philippians 2:12,13.

bound to love Him who is infinitely lovely. We owe supreme allegiance to Him whose authority is supreme. Since we can only value something properly when we value it according to its proper worth, God, being of infinite worth, can only be valued properly when we value Him above all else. Therefore, it is not only a conscious disaffection towards God that proves our depravity, but also the lack of a supreme affection for Him.

John Owen has rightly observed that "where God is not loved above all, He is not loved at all."[85] While it is true that none do love God perfectly in this life, we must still love Him truly. And we only love Him truly, when we love Him supremely; that is, love Him above all else, with all our heart, soul, mind and strength. To love God supremely is not a height that is obtained by a few privileged saints, it is the minimum that God requires of us if we are to call ourselves Christians. To love anything else supremely is idolatry. David Tappan explains,

> Since God, on account of His transcendent excellence
> and worth, is entitled to our supreme affection; it follows
> that no regard to Him can be proper and acceptable,
> which does not far exceed our love to any other object.
> If therefore a person possessed some degree of respect to
> God, but at the same time regarded the world with still
> higher esteem and affection; the former would be justly
> accounted, as nothing, as vanity, and a lie. For nothing
> merits the name of love and homage to the Supreme,
> but that which treats Him as supremely glorious, and
> accordingly gives Him the supremacy, yea, the entire
> possession of the heart.[86]

A subordinate love for God, then, does not constitute the height of our duty toward Him, but rather the depth of our depravity. Where this supreme love for God is lacking, so too is all of our obligation towards Him.

Make no mistake, if we love God, it is not because of any virtue of

---

[85] John Owen, *The Works of John Owen, D. D., Vol. VII* (New York: Robert Carter and Brothers, 1852; original 1676), 463.
[86] David Tappan, *Sermons on Important Subjects by the Late Rev. David Tappan, D. D.* (Boston: W. Hillard and Lincoln & Edmand, 1807), 161.

our own, but because of His gracious work in our hearts. This work is not only commenced but sustained and carried to completion by His almighty power. At the same time, our love for God is an art, with rules and principles that require not only human skill, but also diligent pursuit. Failure to recognize the biblical balance between grace and duty, divine sovereignty and human responsibility, produces either apathy on the one hand or self-righteousness on the other. The over-emphasis of the former shows an indifference to God by not rendering to Him a diligent use of all our faculties (heart, soul, mind and strength), which always spring into action wherever true love for God exist. The overemphasis of the latter shows an indifference to God by an over-preoccupation with ourselves and our own abilities. The first, by neglecting responsibility, cannot be God-focused, because the right consideration of God always compels a radical response. The other, by focusing mainly on duty, has lost sight of God altogether, and is equally self-focused.

Our consumer nature is always dithering between the two extremes where self hopes to retain control – self-gratifying antinomianism, and self-righteous legalism. And since both have a common source in the old nature, the believer must crucify the flesh in both its good and evil forms. Like typical consumers, we have expressed the benefits of coming to God, while erroneously imagining that the necessity of loving God supremely is somehow diminished by the doctrine of justification by grace alone, through faith alone. Justification does not eliminate the need for good works. It is the pathway towards them. For God must accept our person before He will accept our works.[87] The fact that these works are imperfect does not render them less acceptable, so long as they are done by faith,[88] and in the name of the One who also justifies our person by faith.

Justification is a judicial act whereby God declares the sinner righteous. It makes right our relation towards God's law, and if the law no longer condemns us, we shall not perish in our sins. But the believer's life does not end at justification, it only begins. God relates to us on more than a legal basis. In justification God changes our legal standing. In regeneration and sanctification, He removes the pollution of sin and changes our heart as

---

[87] Genesis 4:4.
[88] Hebrews 11:4.

well. J.C. Ryle describes the necessary of a change in both our heart as well as our standing, before we can consider ourselves in a truly blessed state,

> No one ever reached heaven without a renewed heart as well as forgiveness, without the Spirit's grace as well as the blood of Christ, without a meetness for eternal glory as well as a title. The one is just as necessary as the other......Justification gives us our title to heaven, and boldness to enter in. Sanctification gives us our meetness for heaven, and prepares us to enjoy it when we dwell there.[89]

Edward Bickersteth agrees when he writes,

> The title to glory is Christ's work, out of us, the meetness for glory is from the work of the Spirit of Christ in us.[90]

While the legalist opposes the work of Christ without by claiming the work of the Spirit within as his own, the antinomian opposes the work of Christ without by claiming the work of the Spirit within as optional. The first mistakes the ground of salvation, the latter rejects the fruit of salvation. The first is false for commingling justification and sanctification, the latter is false for separating them and allowing them to exist one without the other.

The work within and the work without are to be received on their own merits, without the one excluding the other. For if the premise of one's soteriology requires either a denial or neglect of any of its other parts, it is a scheme resulting not from the work of God in the soul, but from a deficient view of His glory. Because of this two-fold change, we not only rejoice in the hope of the glory of God because of our justification,[91] but we also rejoice in our tribulation, knowing that tribulation produces

---

[89] J C Ryle, *Holiness* (London: James Clark and Co., 1956, reprint), 30-31.
[90] Edward Bickersteth, *The Chief Concerns of Man for Time and Eternity* (London: R. B. Seeley and W. Burnside, 1831), 298.
[91] Romans 5:1,2.

sanctification.[92] James also encourages us to "count it all joy when ye fall into divers temptations."[93] And what is it that he believes will motivates us to count it all joy? Is it because, as difficult as our present circumstances may be, we have the highest standing possible before the One who matters the most? As wonderful a truth as this is, James presents another motivation for such joy, "knowing this, that the trying of your faith worketh patience. But let patience have her perfect work, that ye may be perfect and entire wanting nothing."[94] And why does the prospect of sanctification bring such joy to the child of God, even amid trials and tribulation? Because those whose nature has been changed, and with the eye of faith behold the alluring brightness of His glory, must look very joyfully upon the prospect of displaying that glory with a life transformed more and more into the likeness of such a glorious Being.

The sphere of this display of glory is not limited to the spiritual realm of the heavenly places, but also includes the present physical realm, and reaches even to our bodies. "For ye are bought with a price: therefore glorify God in your body, and in your spirit, which are God's."[95] Salvation is not only purchased for us objectively in justification. Its reach concurs with its price and extends subjectively into our lives as well. Therefore, the highest joy of the Christian comes not only from being counted righteous, but also from being made righteous. This is the sentiment of all of God's children towards both justification and sanctification. One can denounce either self-righteousness or self-indulgence all they want, but so long as they allow the other, self still reigns supreme.

Sanctification is as impossible apart from the basis of justification by grace alone, through faith alone, as justification is apart from its fruits of righteousness in our lives through the Spirit. For the same gospel that warns against including works in our justification,[96] also warns against excluding them in our walk of sanctification.[97] J. J. Van Oosterzee says,

---

[92] Romans 5:3,4.

[93] James 1:2.

[94] James 1:3,4.

[95] 1 Corinthians 6:20.

[96] Ephesians 2:9; Titus 3:5.

[97] Ephesians 2:10, Titus 3:8.

Justification and sanctification must as little be confounded one with another, as arbitrarily separated.[98]

A sure test of an unregenerate heart is the exclusion of either of these two doctrines from one's practice or creed. Thomas Guthrie warns of this danger,

> Yet, if there is need to warn against trusting to their own works for salvation or fixing their hopes on any but the Lamb of God, which taketh away the sins of the world, there is probably as much need to warn others against a more pleasant but equally fatal error – this, namely, that they can be true without being working Christians.[99]

Thomas Scott also confirmed this two-fold danger when he warned,

> Nor is it prudent to represent all the danger to lie on one side, when the opposite extreme is equally fatal.[100]

Being declared righteous does not exempt us from right acting. Our right standing does not eliminate the responsibility for right walking. God gives us right standing in order to start us walking.

> "If ye know that He is righteous, ye know that every one that doeth righteousness is born of Him."[101]

> "Little children, let no man deceive you: he that doeth righteousness is righteous, even as He is righteous."[102]

---

[98] J. J. Van Oosterzee, *Christian Dogmatics* (London: Hodder and Stoughton, 1874), 654.

[99] Thomas Guthrie, *Man and the Gospel and Our Father's Business* (New York: Robert and Brothers, 1876, 381.

[100] Thomas Scott, *Scott's Family Bible* (Philadelphia: William Woodward, 1818), Philippians 3:19.

[101] 1 John 2:29.

[102] 1 John 3:7.

Whether the righteousness is imparted or imputed, the source is still the same. It is Christ's righteousness alone that is the grounds of our standing before God. This verse only states that those who stand before Him with an imputed righteousness, to some degree, also possess an imparted righteousness. Whether righteousness be imputed or imparted, it is still the righteousness of Christ. He who lacks the latter, proves that he is not a recipient of the former, because none can receive salvation while refusing the goal to which it leads, conformity to the image of Christ.[103]

Sanctification is not simply getting use to one's justification, it is a participation in the Divine nature.[104] So the objection of those who cry out, "I seek Christ, not sanctification", is a contradiction in terms. For all who are free to pick and choose among the saving benefits of Christ, do not seek Christ, but only their consumer preferences. Christ is not a marketplace that allows us to choose whatever gratifying goods we prefer, while refusing the rest. We must receive all or none.

"But of Him are ye in Christ Jesus, Who of God is made unto us wisdom, and righteousness and sanctification, and redemption."[105] While the antinomian seeks an exemption from imparted righteousness, contenting himself with imputed righteousness alone, the legalist finds satisfaction in his imparted righteousness without the humbling reality that except for imputed righteousness, even his imparted righteousness would be rejected by God as "filthy rags."[106] But if the end of the process is glorification,[107] we cannot be satisfied with either our justification or our sanctification, but must constantly look forward to the consummation of our redemption, and in the expectation of this, wait for our perfect satisfaction. "I shall be satisfied, when I awake, with Thy likeness."[108]

Justification is only a step to a higher end in our relationship to God. He who rests content with only the reception of this, shows that he seeks no further end. He has received that which is consistent with self-love; therefore, he lacks motivation for anything more. While those who make

---

[103] 1 Peter 1:9, Romans 8:29, Ephesians 1:4, 12.

[104] 2 Peter 1:4-11.

[105] 1 Corinthians 1:30.

[106] Isaiah 64:6.

[107] Romans 8:29-30.

[108] Psalm 17:15.

sanctification all that they seek from God in salvation miss that which God seeks above all else, His own glory, those who make justification all that they want out of salvation also miss that which God desires above all else – to display that glory through the regenerating and sanctifying work of the Spirit.

Nor can any claim exclusion from duty based on a positional sanctification. Union with Christ is central in sanctification. But this does not rest in a work done outside us but involves something within us. It "is Christ in you" who is "the hope of glory."[109] "He who hath the Son hath life."[110] While all believers are sanctified in principle, based on their union with Christ, this state must show itself in a life of holiness, which is unattainable without constant and diligent, although ever God dependent, effort. "For without Me ye can do nothing."[111] As is evident from the history of the nation of Israel, and confirmed by the letters written to the churches,[112] God will suffer no rivals in the soul wherein He dwells and that He has sanctified for Himself. To be set apart by grace as the people of God entails great responsibility. He sets us apart, so that we might set Him apart in our hearts.[113]

"Thou shalt worship no other god, for the Lord, whose name is Jealous, is a jealous God."[114] God, "whose name is Jealous," imparts grace only in such a way that reveals His name (character), and not in such a way that invalidates it, or eliminates any aspect of His holy nature. Such a god only exists in the mind of the consumer. For the God of the Bible does not impart grace to console its recipients in their worship of idols. He redeems us for the same reason that He created us – for His own glory. That glory is manifested wherever His multifaceted perfections are put on

---

[109] Colossians 1:27.

[110] 1 John 5:12.

[111] John 15:5.

[112] James 4:4 – 5, Revelation 2:4 – 5.

[113] "In the Scripture, we see the price paid, the curse borne, in order that those who are redeemed should be brought into the liberty of the sons of God, a liberty which may paradoxically be called slavery to God. The whole point of this redemption is that sin no longer has dominion; the redeemed are those saved to do the will of their Master" Leon Morris, *The Apostolic preaching of the Cross* (Grand Rapids: Eerdmans Publishing Company, 1956), 59.

[114] Exodus 34:14.

display, and not when they are contradicted by our lifestyle and practice. This is why God is glorified in the saint's ultimate glorification. He will restore His image in us in order that He may display His glory through us. O glorious day!

Nor can any be excluded from his present responsibilities with the hope that glorification is yet future, and therefore sanctification should be left for another life, since none are perfect in the present. While God is glorified in our ultimate glorification,[115] we are not to wait for heaven for this process to begin. God's central purpose in our present lives is our sharing in His holiness.[116] "For this is the will of God, even your sanctification."[117] Sanctification is glorification already begun, glorification is sanctification perfected. That cannot be perfected which has never begun. He who hopes to experience the end, will likewise rejoice in experiencing the means by which he advances ever closer towards that end. Therefore, he must accept as his highest privilege the responsibility to love God with all his heart, soul, mind and strength; otherwise, he deceives himself as to his real hopes.

Presumption, being a groundless expectation, is always opposed to real hope. The real hope of glorification in the future, moves one towards glorification in the present. Such is the sanctifying power of hope.

> "Beloved, now we are the sons of God, and it doth not yet appear what we shall be; but we know that when He shall appear we shall be like Him, for we shall see Him as He is. And every man that hath this hope in him purifies himself, even as He is pure."[118]

To test the reality of the work of God in the soul, one must only show that the work has begun, and not that it is already perfected. And the work that has begun in the soul will constantly be perfecting itself through the power of the indwelling Spirit.

Every imaginable consumer-driven excuse that we could possibly

---

[115] John 17:22.

[116] Hebrews 12:10 – 11.

[117] 1 Thessalonians 4:3.

[118] 1 John 3:2 – 3.

employ, to exempt those customers whom we desire to either attract or retain from that duty which they find repulsive, reveals our own disdain for the highest enjoyment and present employment of the children of God. We cannot successfully conceal the height of man's duty from any present or potential customer, without equally revealing our own aversion to the holiness of God that compels such duty. Elizabeth Rundle Charles describes all such methods as counterproductive to the real mission of the church,

> The church loses her power of attraction when she relinquishes her atmosphere of repulsion. The profession which will not offend the careless cannot teach the earnest. If the salt has lost its savour, it cannot heal the bitter waters.[119]

The real reason men do not believe is because "men love darkness rather than light, because their deeds were evil."[120] The solution for church growth is not found in diming the light, for the light of the gospel both attracts and repels.[121] That part of the gospel that many find repulsive, is the very thing that the others find attractive. That which is "the savour of death" unto some, is "the savour of life" unto others.[122] To the degree that we reach our goal of repelling none, we forfeit that power that is necessary to attract any. The church's salt has lost its savor once its light is accommodated to the darkness.

---

[119] Elizabeth Rundle Charles, *Tales and Sketches of Christian Life in Different Lands and Ages* (New York: Robert Carter and Brothers, 1865), 27.
[120] John 3:21.
[121] 1 Corinthians 1:18; 2 Corinthians 2:16.
[122] 2 Corinthians 2:16.

CHAPTER 3

The Depth of Depravity, A Subordinate Love for God

Hath a nation changed their gods, which are yet no gods? But My people have changed their Glory for that which does not profit.....For My people have committed two evils; they have forsaken Me the fountain of living waters, and hewn them out cisterns, broken cisterns, that can hold no water.

Jeremiah 2:11,13

"How prone mankind are to place religion in anything else rather than in the state of the heart, and to acknowledge the kingdom of God in any form, provided it does not assert a supremacy over the affections."[123]

Samuel Shaw

I f our highest duty is to love God supremely, then to love ourselves or anything else more than God must be the greatest evil imaginable. The evilness of sin consists in its despising God. In fact, sin, in its very essence, is the displacement of God from the supreme place in our affections and replacing Him with something vastly inferior. All sin is an attack against the nature of God. "No man can serve two masters; for either he will hate

---

[123] Samuel Shaw, *Emmanuel* (Glasgow: printed for William Collins; 1829), x.

the one and love the other; or else he will hold to the one, and despise the other. Ye cannot serve God and mammon."[124] Therefore, the depth of our depravity is not simply that we love ourselves supremely, but that in so doing we despise God, the fountain living water.

Whatever it is that we love or delight in more than God, in effect, becomes our god. Pride makes a god of self, covetousness makes a god of money, and lust makes a god of the flesh. To esteem anything more important than God is an affront, a contempt and an open defiance of Him. By our actions we declare that there is something greater than God; something we set up in the place of God, and we render to it that very esteem that belongs to God alone.

Our lives will either magnify Him by declaring His supremacy to all things, or they will insult Him by proclaiming that there is another. Whatever value other things may have, God is infinitely beyond all estimation. Therefore, we only value Him properly when we count Him inestimable. By permitting anything to interfere with His claim to supreme affection, we proclaim our dissatisfaction with the "One needful thing."[125]

The absurdity of exalting any part of God's creation above Him in our affections becomes obvious only to those who recognize His infinite worth. While all recognize a general depravity among men, it is man's blindness to God's inestimable worth that renders him insensible to the depth of his own depravity. This blindness continues on all those who call on the name of Christ but make light of sin. A true sense of the sinfulness of sin always accompanies a true sense of the holiness of God. A true sense of our depravity is revealed not by answering the question "Do we sin?", for few would be so bold as to claim perfection. Nor by answering the question "Why do we sin?" But the true sense of the depths of our depravity is gained by answering the question "Why do we not take our sins seriously?" Such a lack of the seriousness of sin is seen in much of our evangelism where sin is shown as serious only in reference to the consequences to man. In such a case, the goal is not to reveal, but to conceal the alluring brightness of His glory. To make light of sin proves that one has exalted other things above God, for exalting God in our affections always involves a corresponding loathing of all things that are contrary to Him.

---

[124] Matthew 6:24.
[125] Luke 10:42.

The absurdity of exalting other things above Him becomes even more apparent once we consider that all these idols, whether wealth, pleasures or honor, are merely broken cisterns. They require a great deal of exertion to hew, but in the end, hold no satisfying water. Those who would view the depths of depravity as consisting of nothing more than an outright hatred of God, rather than also including a subordinate love for Him, mistake His glorious nature.[126]

Many would gladly cherish God as a secondary love, if it would not disturb the pursuit of their primary love. And the consumer-driven church not only offers such a god who will not disturb our most precious pursuits, but one who exist to promote the various gratifications of its customers. Our delight in these counterfeit offers reveal that we derive little satisfaction from God, the fountain of living water. This is why the church forsakes Him for the polluted streams of the world. All such wanderings from God can only be in pursuit of idols. And the only thing we will find by leaving the fountain are broken cisterns. Therefore, it is to the preservation of true joy, and not to its exclusion, that we forsake not the Fount of all delight.

The objects that the world seeks (riches, honor, influence, significance and pleasure) are corruptible crowns. They are for but a moment, and comparably nothings. It is only as the church recognizes the ultimate and enduring value of Christ, that it will joyfully suffer the loss of all things, including life itself, to gain Him.[127] He who has found the pearl of great price, willingly and joyfully sells all he has that he might purchase it.[128] He is thus rendered incapable of finding his highest satisfaction in the transient joys of the world. Having found something of far greater value, he easily parts with the lesser.

Our unwillingness to break with the world stems from our failure to recognize the vanity of the world. Our failure to recognize the vanity of the world stems from our failure to recognize, by way of contrast, the majesty of God. The more we recognize the superiority and excellency of heavenly things, the more we will recognize the inferiority and vanity of earthly

---

[126] James 4:4.

[127] Philippians 3:8.

[128] Matthew 13:45 – 46.

things, and their insufficiency to satisfy apart from God. God has declared the material world as good, but vain when pursued apart from Him.

The enticing lure of the world on our affections decreases to the degree that the perception of our privileges and inheritance in Christ increases. No one can accurately comprehend or appreciate the spiritual realities that are his in Christ while remaining enticed by the world. To the degree that our hearts are turned towards God, they will be diverted from the praise, pleasures and riches offered by the world. Faith, by perceiving a greater portion in God, overcomes the world.[129] Since the world is so diametrically opposed to God, the only possible response of those who love God is to oppose the world. James describes the intensity of this opposition when he asks: "Know ye not that the friendship of the world is enmity with God?"[130] *The Illustrated Bible Dictionary* captures the essence of James' thought when it states,

> The love of a Christian for God, acts with the expulsive power of a new affection: it makes it abhorrent for him to set his affections any longer upon this world.....A man who has come to experience the higher love for God, and for Christ and his brethren, must abandon the lower love of all that is contaminated by the spirit of the world.[131]

Our opposition to the world must be as radical as the sharp contrast between God and the world. To be at peace with the world is to be an enemy of God. Failure to actively resist the world is a passive resistance and hatred of God Himself. The pendulum of our affections cannot move in one direction without moving from the opposite direction. Therefore, all of our professed love for God is a lie, if our hearts go after the world. "If any man love the world, the love of the Father is not in him."[132] "It is impossible", says William Jones, "to know the things of God, while

---

[129] 1 John 5:4.

[130] James 4:4.

[131] World, *The Illustrated Bible Dictionary, Vol., 3* (Wheaton: Tyndale House Publishers, 1980), 1656.

[132] 1 John 2:15.

our hearts are set upon the world. Ignorance of God will cherish earthly affections."[133] "God gave them up unto vile affections" who "did not like to retain God in their knowledge."[134]

There can be no greater insult than to be dissatisfied with He who is of infinite worth, simply because we fail to possess that which ultimately has no value, the world and all that it offers. Not only when compared with God, but even when compared to our own souls, the world appears worthless. "For what is a man profited, if he shall gain the whole world, and lose his own soul?"[135] So then, he who has an infinite portion, will gladly part with the finite. He who has an infinite inheritance, will count himself infinitely blessed, with or without the finite.

Men can see an evilness in the world as it goes contrary to their own welfare, but they also see an enticing beauty. The world's utter depravity is just as impossible for man to see as the total depravity of his own heart. Unless our vision is rectified to see the beauty of the Lord, we cannot see the corresponding trifling nature of the world. To the degree that we see any beauty in the world ("the lust of the flesh, and the lust of the eyes, and the pride of life"),[136] we despise that part of God which it opposes. Pleasures, possessions and self are deified when the world becomes the object of our affections. Whereas, the moment God becomes our Object, the world becomes our abject.

Worldliness, which is the inordinate love of the things of the world, can only be remedied by a whole-hearted and genuine love for God. This genuine love for God can only exist where the corrupt love of self has been subdued. Man's corrupt self-love is the essence of his depravity. He is his own idol. He has become his own idol by preferring himself to God. This choice is not between a good and a better object, but between two contrary objects. Since man's heart was turned from God to self in the fall, he now hates that which comes against self, especially God.

In order to serve the true God, our hearts must first be turned from self back to God. Our affections must be turned from the love of self before

---

[133] William Jones, *The Theological, Philosophical and Miscellaneous Works of the Late Rev. William Jones Vol. V* (London: F. and C. Rivington, 1801), 33.

[134] Romans 1:26,28.

[135] Matthew 16:26.

[136] 1 John 2:16.

they will love the Creator. We must be made holy before we can love the Holy One. This change man cannot effect. And the reason isn't because God is not lovely enough of an object, but because of the blindness of man to perceive such a loveliness, and the tendency of his heart to always be centered upon himself. Once centered upon himself, he lacks that motive of love toward God which should govern all his actions, thereby making true virtue impossible. He is totally depraved, because there is a total absence of that which should control all his actions. Far from acting as wicked as he can, he now seeks to replace his greatest duty with the performance of duties that center on self; and obscure the enormity of his greatest evil with the avoidance of sins that are repulsive to self, all the while excluding God as the primary consideration for his actions.[137]

According to John Howe, the doctrine of total depravity does not negate a subordinate self-love, which God has also commanded from his subjects:

> For when God's law requires us to love our neighbor as ourselves, it implies there is a love which we owe to ourselves; not that inordinate self-love which excludes both love to God and our neighbor; but such as is subordinate to the one and co-ordinate with the other.[138]

The postmodern church, however, is especially deceived on this point. It is quick to receive and promote a man-centered gospel that allows self-love to reign supreme. The true gospel, on the other hand, is not good news to the man in love with himself. Its design is the very opposite of what drives the post-modern church – to humble man to the dust, by placing God at the center, to the exclusion of all else. Those who endorse man's core values would have the opposite effect – the validation of man rather than

---

[137] "Whatsoever is good in a natural man is depraved by a self-end; self-love rules all his actions. He keeps within himself; makes his chief end himself; is a god to himself and God is his idol. This is true of all natural men in the world; they make themselves their great end, and where the end is depraved, the whole course must be wrong." Richard Sibbes, *Divine Meditations and Holy Contemplations* (London: J. Buckland, 1775), 87.

[138] John Howe, *The Works of John Howe, M.A.* (London: The Religious Tract Society, 1872), 404.

God. God has forever linked man's salvation with His own glory.[139] "The design of the gospel is to set forth God in Christ as an amiable Object, as infinitely glorious," says Stephen Charnock.[140]

Is it any wonder that men apply the wrong remedy when they diagnose the wrong disease? From an incorrect diagnosis proceeds a man-centered Christianity that blinds men to the greatness of their supreme obligation, even in the faithful performance of many duties. It also blinds them to the greatest evil, even in the avoidance of many evils. All because self is really intended, while God is only pretended. The words of J C Ryle confirm the cause of the primary misconceptions of consumer-driven Christianity today:

> I believe there are very few errors and false doctrine of which the beginning may not be traced up to unsound views about the corruption of human nature.[141]

The consumer-driven church assumes that the primary problem is not with the customer, but with the message and how it is presented. They assume that if we could somehow make Christianity more marketable and attractive, then the lost would simply have no inner aversion towards Christianity. Coherent with the need to satisfy its present customers is the need not to offend any potential customer. Thus, what follows is the need to conform to the world's opinion of what religion ought to be. The only way to remove the aversion is by conversion. When it is Christianity that does the converting, the lost have no reason to convert. Convert from what? By its actions, the church has already proved to the world that the problem lies not with the depravity of man, but with the foolishness of the message and method of the cross. The church differs nothing from the world when it calls them to all those things that the cross calls them from.

The deceits of Satan are so subtle that Christianity can take on many false forms. Yet all these forms have the same tendency (the tendency of

---

[139] Ephesians 1:5 – 6, 14.

[140] Stephen Charnock, *The Doctrine of regeneration* (Philadelphia: Presbyterian Board of Publication, 1840), 129.

[141] J C Ryle, *Knots Untied* (Moscow, Idaho: Charles Nolan Publishers, 2000; original, 1874), 356.

Satan himself), which is the removal of God from the place of supremacy, and the establishment of self in His place. Whether man trusts in the sufficiency of his own works to merit God's favor, uses God as a means to his own ends, or comes to God with no desire to render complete obedience to His will, the results are the same, self still reigns supreme.

As innocent as the choosing of oneself above God may appears to man, it is this very act that constitutes the depth of his depravity. For in choosing oneself, God is rejected. Whether as Mediator (by trusting in his own works), as End (by making himself the end and God the means), or as Sovereign (by determining to what extent he should submit to God), some part, and therefore all of God, is rejected. To retain the right to choose to what extent or how much God controls our life is to retain full control of our life. The deciding factor in all these cases is not God, but us. If we do not know Him as Mediator, End and Sovereign, we do not know Him as God.

The only cure for our depravity must be a supreme love for God, whereby He unties our hearts from ourselves, and brings them back to Himself as their true center. But without a thorough recognition of his total depravity, man will not go to the fountain of living water provided for the cleansing of his defilement, as well as the only satisfaction for his sins. Instead, he will seek a lesser cure. One that merely removes some outer symptoms, changing the outward form, but allowing the disease to fester unhindered within. Total depravity requires a total cure. One that we cannot apply ourselves, because our disease has already killed us.[142]

Justification and the forgiveness of sins alone are not sufficient to cure the depravity of man's heart. As essential as they are, they do not define the totality of man's salvation. Something must happen within us, as well as without us. Man must be born again. New life must be generated. To counter the depraved nature, a new and opposite nature must be imparted.

Those who do not see sin in the heart as the cause of all of man's ills, will not see the urgency for the new birth, and focus exclusively on the consequences of the guilt of sin as the real problem of man. We must show man both his need for forgiveness and the new birth. Simply ignoring the depraved nature of the human heart, while promoting the free forgiveness of sins that is offered in Christ, cannot be without the most

---

[142] Ephesians 2:1.

serious consequences. No matter how burdened one feels over his sins, it is nothing but self-idolatry, unless one desires the new heart that accompanies forgiveness. One must be burdened with himself, and not merely with the consequences of his actions against himself. False presumptions of forgiveness will always follow the false preaching of forgiveness. "He who is not acquainted with God's holiness and purity, who knows not sin's desert and sinfulness, known nothing of forgiveness,"[143] says Owen. This more marketable form of Christianity may produce a more populous and popular Christianity, but in the end a more depraved one; one that reflects so unworthily on the glory of God that it becomes a deformity which He cannot bear to look upon.[144] As the Laodicean succeeded, like no other church, in becoming relevant to man, so it also succeeded in making itself more odious to God.

---

[143] John Owen, The Works of John Owen, D. D. Vol. VI (London and Edinburgh: Johnstone and Hunter, 1851), 394.
[144] Isaiah 1:11 – 14.

CHAPTER 4

Consumer-Driven Christianity Defined

Because that, when they knew God, they glorified Him not as God, neither were thankful; but became vain in their imaginations, and their foolish heart was darkened. Professing themselves to be wise, they became fools, and changed the glory of the uncorruptible God into an image made like to corruptible man.

Romans 1:21, 22, 23

For the time is coming when people will not endure sound teaching, but having itching ears they will accumulate for themselves teachers to suit their own likings.

2 Timothy 4:3 RSV

Romans 1:21 – 33, by describing the predisposition of the depraved, reveal the tendency of all depravity. The natural and universal tendency of man's heart is to "change the glory of the uncorruptible God into an image made like to corruptible man;"[145] and to "change the truth of God into a lie, and worship and serve the creature more than

---

[145] Romans 1:23.

the Creator."[146] Consumer-driven Christianity exists primarily to satisfy the needs and desires of the creature above the desires and designs of the Creator. It is essentially idolatrous for the preferences of the creature to dictate the structure of his religion or the form of his god.

Man, in his depraved state, finds it easier and preferable to serve a god of his own making, than to serve the God of the Scriptures. If he does not worship a graven image, he will set up something above God in his affections. Even more, he will turn the true God into an idol of his own imagination. God becomes an idol in our imagination when we form and embrace thoughts of Him that are totally unworthy or contrary to His glorious essence. "Thou thoughtest that I was altogether such an one as thyself,"[147] is the fatal error of the city of man.

This form of idolatry is always the most deceptive form of them all. For while we may flatter ourselves with the idea that unlike the false religions and the non-religious we believe in the true God, we fail to consider that inaccurate belief in the true God is still idolatry. It is not the name of your God that matters most, it is the God behind the name. In Scripture, God's name refers to His nature and character. To love His name,[148] therefore, is to love His manifest perfections. "His name alone is excellent,"[149] not because He choose the best combination of syllables by which to form it, but because His attributes are most excellent. His name, void of a conscious acknowledgement of His attributes, is not the proper object of worship, but an idol of our own imagination. The true God, stripped of even one of His attributes, becomes a false god. Simply giving the right name to our erroneous concept of God does not make us any less idolaters.

While it is true that our knowledge of God is only in part, there is a great difference between partial knowledge and knowledge that is fundamentally wrong. There is also a great difference between partial knowledge and willful ignorance. As the Greeks fashioned their gods to resemble themselves, we too could fashion God to resemble something other than He is. Our love for this false conception is mistaken for love

---

[146] Romans 1:25.
[147] Psalms 50:21.
[148] Psalms 5:11.
[149] Psalms 148:13.

for God. But a misguided knowledge of God implies a misguided love for Him. Although we cannot know God in His very essence, we must know enough to draw off our affections from the world, ourselves, and everything else that might exalt itself against the knowledge of God. If we do not perceive His preeminence to all things, we will only come with our own preeminence in view, and so be drawn to Him solely for our own personal benefit.

While it is an abomination to carve an image to worship in the place of God, it is blasphemy to conceive of God as such a one as ourselves. It is one thing to dethrone God for another, but it is the utmost pride to usurp His throne by conforming Him to our own image. We are self-idolaters whenever God exists in our mind only to promote our self-interest; when we enlist Him in the service of our almighty self. He is dethroned in our heart when He exist for us, and not we for Him; when His primary role is that of a servant, and not of a sovereign; when we believe that He is somehow impressed by our service, and therefore indebted to us to act on our behalf for all that we have done for Him.

Is it any wonder that such a religion that places man at the center would likewise flourish among men? The secret of attracting potential customers to any religion is to offer them the religion of their choice. The consumer-driven church is especially set up to accommodate this counterfeit religion. And like all counterfeit religion, unless it gives some resemblance of the true, it deceives none but the willfully blind. Therefore, it must proclaim the Christian God, while at the same time denouncing His supremacy with its insistence on the preeminence of man. It is impossible to view the true God through such lenses. We cannot promote the true knowledge of God while holding out to the world its choicest idols, albeit in a more refined form.

Men desire to know God only insofar as they do not have to glorify Him as God. In other words, they desire to know a god who also worships and serves man. As man once thought of the universe as centered around the earth, and the stars were concerned with nothing more than to reveal the fate of man, so man continues to think that God centers around himself, his trivial desires and ambitions; whereas, the Bible reveals that man is only a part of God's great purpose, and that all things center around God. Although the Bible declares that God is our helper,[150] when this secondary function becomes primary, as it does in the consumer-driven church, we cease to worship the God of the Bible. There are many statements about God in the Bible, which, while true in themselves, if taken as the whole become false. The popular god that is worshipped today is not the God of the Bible, but merely the god that our consumer nature wished were in the Bible; a god who is an easy sell to those who are likewise supremely in love with themselves.

We "change the truth of God into a lie," when we preach a god who is more devoted to us, than His own glory. When man becomes the center, we "worship and serve the creature, more than the Creator." We only worship the Creator when we choose Him as our supreme good, and, as a consequence, resign all earthly idols. The true worshipper's love for God excludes all other lovers. He not only loves God more, he loves Him alone. He loves all men as they bare His image, and all things as coming from His hands and tending towards His glory.

True love for God not only connects all things to Him, it also aligns all our faculties with Him. Stephen Charnock connects all our faculties (understanding, will and affections) when describing the essence of true worship,

> This must be done with understanding (Ps 47:7); with a knowledge and sense of greatness, goodness, and wisdom. It is also an act of the will, whereby the soul adores and reverences His majesty, is ravished with His amiableness, embraces His goodness, enters itself into an intimate communion with this most lovely object, and pitches all his affections upon Him.[151]

Unless we value Him above self and our happiness, we will only love Him for ourselves, and make Him a means to our happiness, instead of our chief end. When we make ourselves the end and God the means, we dishonor Him by taking His rightful place. Herein lies the proof and

---

[150] Psalms 54:4.

[151] Stephen Charnock, *The Existence and Attributes of God* (Grand Rapids: Baker Books, 1997; original, 1853), 222 – 223.

power of our self-deception; not that we do not love God, but that we love Him only in part and for the wrong reasons. God is no longer the One we seek above all things, but the One we seek to obtain all things. Trials are not to prove the genuineness of our faith in God, but our lack thereof. Satan is no longer the one who tempts us to sin, but the one who comes against our happiness. Overcoming Satan is no longer overcoming those things that rebel against God (sin, the flesh and the world), or attack His glory, but overcoming those things that attack our success and happiness.

Contrary to the opinion of the consumer-driven church, real faith does not insure our success in the eyes of the world, it rather renders such success irrelevant. "But what things were gain to me, those I counted loss for Christ."[152] This truth is all but incomprehensible to those who confuse their greatest loss with their greatest gain. The objection that this truth will only produce a group of underachievers can only be raised by those who count the opinion of man as a greater motivation to love and good works than the esteem of God. All who hold to such an objection are the real underachievers, because this opinion renders one incapable of doing any good work at all, which works can only be done purely for the glory of God, and not for the recognition that we hope to receive from men.

If you love God simply because He loves and blesses you, then "what reward have ye? Do not even the publicans the same?"[153] This is the very same love of which Satan falsely accused Job.[154] If this is the case with us, then all of our worship is self-worship, all of our service is self-serving, and all of our obedience is self-seeking. Thomas Brooks expressed these same thoughts when he wrote,

> Few follow Him for love, but for the loaves (John 6:26). Few follow Him for His inward excellencies, but many follow Him for their outward advantage; few follow Him that they may be made good by Him, but many follow Him that they may be made great by Him.[155]

---

[152] Philippians 3:7.

[153] Matthew 5:46.

[154] Job 1:9.

[155] Thomas Brooks, *The Complete Works of Thomas Brooks, Vol. 2* (Edinburgh: James Nichol, 1866), 426.

Selfish men will give their lives for the ministry, for a church, to study the Bible, to do good works, or to the outward form of godliness, because self can always find some advantage in all these things. The rich young ruler is proof that the flesh not only expresses itself in doing evil, but can also express itself in the diligent pursuit of that which is relatively good. All men, to a greater or lesser degree, are subject to a common grace that is both superficial and transient, modifying the actions without changing the nature. The results of this within Christianity is a self-centered spirituality that makes one study to appear wise, pursue ministry for applause, give to be seen, and attend church or abstain from outward sins to appear respectable. This type of spirituality always connects holy things with self; therefore, it is self-worship. The problem is not that God is left out, but that self is put above. God is not loved more than self, but because of self.

Self-centered spiritually could be even more of an abomination to God than self-gratifying sensuality. For while self-gratifying sensuality declares that there are pleasures to be had that are greater than God, self-centered spirituality, by making God a means to some other end in religion – namely self, declares that self is a greater end to pursue in religion than God. While both affirm that the creature is greater than the Creator, the former affirms that we exist for the creature, and the latter that the Creator exist for us.

God alone must be loved with all our heart, soul, mind and strength. While we are commanded to love our neighbor as we love ourselves, to love them, or anything else, with that supreme love due solely to God is idolatry. It should follow, then, that to love ourselves with that same supreme love is equally idolatrous. And if we can love ourselves too much, then we can equally love our neighbor too much when we idolize any man. "If any man come to Me, and hate not his father, and mother, and wife, and children, and brethren, and sisters, yea, and his own life also, he cannot be My disciple."[156] The word hate, in this context, means to value God infinitely more. It follows, then, that any love for God that flows solely out of love for ourselves, cannot be that supreme love which God requires. You cannot love God above self, if self is the sole basis of your love for Him. "If I make God's love to me, the foundation of my love to Him," says Seth Williston, "I make myself more than God; I make all His

---

[156] Luke 14:26.

worthiness of my love, to consist in His regard for me, and attention to my happiness."[157]

John's statement in 1 John 4:19, "We love Him because He first loved us," does not imply that we love Him because we perceive that He first loved us. For this, by definition, is selfish love. Rather, it means that our love for God is possible only because of His unmerited and unconditional love manifested in the sacrifice of His Son on our behalf. We do not receive this power to love because we now have the example of Christ on the cross, for this would indeed be salvation by example of sacrifice, rather than salvation by His sacrifice. We, in our depraved state, are incapable of agape, whether toward God or man. But He, on the basis of His sacrificial love, now implants love of like kind as a fruit of His Spirit in our hearts.[158]

The love that was "poured out in our hearts by the Holy Spirit" was not merely a reciprocal love (based solely on the recognition of the good that was shown to us), for all men, to a higher or lesser degree, already possess this type of love. Man, even in his depraved state, may be moved to a superficial and self-centered love towards a deity upon hearing of his love for him and desire to do him good. If this is all the drawing power of the gospel, then it is not the power of God unto salvation, but only the power of self-love. The love of which all men are incapable, in their depraved state, is a love that places God as its principle Object above self and is non-consumer. Therefore, this love must likewise express itself in sacrificial acts of unconditional kindness toward all men, and not merely towards those with whom we have an amity.

Self-gratification and self-denial are mutually exclusive principles that may dwell together but can never reign together in the same heart. Unless self be denied, Christ can never be truly loved. "Two cities have been formed by two loves;" said Augustine, "the earthly by the love of self, even to the contempt of God; the heavenly by the love of God, even to the contempt of self."[159] Let men keep their sin, pleasures and reputation, without persecutions, and they would gladly keep Christ. There are many

---

[157] Seth Williston, *Sermons on doctrinal and Experimental Subjects* (Hudson: A. Stoddard, 1812), 172.

[158] Romans 5:5; Galatians 5:22.

[159] Augustine, *The Works of Aurelius Augustine,* Vol. II, Book XIV, Chapter 28 (Edinburgh: T and T Clark, 1871), 47.

inhabitants of the city of man who are pretenders to the city of God. Judas loved Christ, but only as a means to obtain money.[160] Simon the sorcerer loved Christ as a means to spiritual power.[161] The rich young ruler loved Christ, but he loved his riches more.[162] He wanted heaven more than hell, but he did not want heaven more than earth. Like the seed sown on the stony ground, many receive the Word with gladness,[163] but for some other end than its own loveliness. The moment Christ competes with self, men would rather forsake Christ, than deny self. Therefore, "when affliction or persecution ariseth for the word's sake, immediately they are offended."[164] Being no more valuable to self, Christ is no longer valuable at all. One may inwardly fall away from Christ while outwardly embracing Him, when he invents a christ whose thoughts rise no higher than the selfish interests of man. William Wilberforce warns of this self-deception when he writes,

> It is deceptive for one to imagine that God only condemns a total rejection of Him. God also will not accept divided affections.[165]

He who is the loveliest Object, when viewed properly, cannot be loved as a means to some other end. God must be loved above the good things that he bestows upon us, and not because of them. John Flavel once said,

> Every man loves the mercies of God, but a saint loves the God of mercies.....not Thine but Thee O Lord, is the motto of a gracious soul; but yet these things serve to blow up the flame of love to God in their hearts.[166]

---

[160] John 12:4-6.

[161] Acts 8:13 – 23.

[162] Matthew 19:16 – 22.

[163] Mark 4:16.

[164] Mark 4:17.

[165] William Wilberforce, *A Practical View of Christianity* (Peabody: Hendrickson, 1996; original, 1797), 85.

[166] John Flavel, *The Whole Works of the Rev. Mr. John Flavel, Vol. IV* (London: W. Baynes and Sons, 1820), 438.

The blessings of God are nothing more than oil to the wheels of our obedience. They are not the motor that drives it. While they serve to make our obedience more delightful, only a proper view of God is what drives it.

Although God blesses us with Himself above all else, we cannot despise even the least of His blessings, including those that are common to all men. It is inconceivable that God would create so many pleasures and delights, only to turn around and say, "do not touch, do not handle."[167] For God "gives us richly all things to enjoy."[168] "Nothing is to be refused if it is received with thanksgiving."[169] But it is through thanksgiving that we give back glory to God for all these things. For true thanksgiving refocuses our eyes from the blessing, back on God, as both the source of every blessing and the real Object of esteem.

All that God bestows is to be received as gifts to be used for His glory. Any ingratitude towards the gift is ingratitude towards the Giver. While we receive the gifts from God, they must not take the place of God, who alone can satisfy. For while we despise none, so we must idolize none. Whether possessions, learning or influence, these are all given as gracious gifts from God.[170] They are not ours to keep by right, for we have not earned them. If God bestows them, it is a sign of His goodness, to be received with thanksgiving and used for His glory. If He withholds them, it is also a sign of His goodness, designed for our ultimate good, as well as His own glory. Therefore, the believer can accept failure as well as success; tribulation as well as comfort; suffering as well as ease. For whenever He deprives us of those things that might ensnare us, it is only because He has chosen to impart something far greater.

The real reason we exalt other things above God, is because our spiritual depravity has blinded us to His true goodness and majesty. The veil over our eyes is our depravity. This depravity, while not hindering us from understanding the word objectively, does subjectively blind our hearts from its spiritual light and beauty. Unless we first come to see the beauty of the Lord, we will never cease to make Him a means to some other end. The true knowledge of God always produces elevated thoughts

---

[167] Colossians 2:21.

[168] 1 Timothy 6:17.

[169] 1 Timothy 4:4.

[170] 1 Corinthians 4:7.

of God and, by contrast, lower thoughts of everything else. We insist on holding to high views of ourselves and other things, only because we are blind to the excellencies of God. The reason we hold to our own greatness is because we are blind to the greatness of God. We fail to see these things, because we have no sight with which to see them. We are blind to them, because our depraved nature is contrary to them. Such spiritual blindness will inevitably lead its possessors away from God and toward a man-centered Christianity, where man's condition is not so bleak, nor his power so impotent.

Man's depravity hinders him from seeing himself as utterly odious and powerless, because he cannot bring himself to acknowledge God as infinitely lovely and powerful, in and of Himself, without reference to man. To say that we were anything but odious implies that there was some loveliness within us that could possibly merit God's love or attract His attention. God is not irresistibly drawn to love us by some force outside of Himself, namely our own loveliness. To say that there was something in us that could merit God's love diminishes from His unconditional and unmerited love and renders it less amazing and more human than divine. To say that we were anything but powerless, invites us to look within, instead of solely without, for that strength which comes from the Lord.

The design of the gospel is to put to shame all human strength so "that no flesh should glory in His presence."[171] Without these discoveries there can be no recovery, for real recovery would not be sought; or at most only a superficial one. Men would simply content themselves in the worship of an idol that they have invented for themselves; one by which they merely become children of a lesser god; one who is truly less amazing. And the higher you exalt man in your theology, the lower your god becomes.

---

[171] 1 Corinthians 1:24 – 29.

CHAPTER 5

A Strong Delusion, Sinners in Zion Warmed

> The sinners in Zion are afraid; fearfulness hath surprised the hypocrites. Who among us shall dwell with the devouring fire? Who among us shall dwell with everlasting burnings?
>
> Isaiah 33:14

Consumer-driven Christianity, like paganism, is essentially idolatrous. The greatest difference being that this form of idolatry is even more offensive to God.[172] Whether it be an openly displayed idol (like the Jews in Jerusalem, Ezek 8), or an internal, spiritual idol (like the Jews in Babylon, Ezek 14), God will not share His glory with another. Those who are set upon offering strange fire before the Lord (that is, contrive some way of serving Him that is more agreeable to the fallen nature of man), do not enhance God's glory in the eyes of the customer, but only that of the customer, and place themselves under God's judgment.[173] God's jealous anger is being kindled against those who seek to rob Him of that glory by placing their supreme affection in something other than Himself – in this case the all absorbing quest for the attention of the consumer even above God Himself. Jealousy in God refers to an indignant and righteous

---

172 Revelations 3:15,16.
173 Numbers 26:61.

determination that His honor should be upheld.[174] Since God's honor is withheld whenever we put the desires of the customer above His will revealed in His word, the consumer-driven church must be dishonoring to God. In just such a way did the children of Israel dishonor God in the Old Testament and were ultimately driven into captivity.

> And ye shall know that I am the Lord: for ye have not walked in My statutes, neither executed My judgments, but have done after the manners of the heathen that are round about you.[175]

Becoming like the world is the sure sign that we have ceased our quest to become like God.

"Certainly, the consequences of following the customs of those around us cannot be so severe in this age of grace," we quickly abject. But the author of Hebrews exhorts us to "have grace, whereby we may serve God acceptably with reverence and godly fear: for our God is a consuming fire."[176] Grace is not antagonistic to godly fear, it produces it. Grace is needed, not to excuse our unacceptable worship, but to enable us all the more to render acceptable worship. Such worship is always accompanied with reverence and godly fear. Neither does faith exclude fear. Faith produces fear, when the Object of faith is the true God. It is the mark of the unbeliever that "there is no fear of God before their eyes."[177] The reason this reverence and fear is lacking in our modern worship is because the true God has been replaced with a god of love that puts man at the center of all of God's activities. Will God give up His will simply because we have no relish for it? Shall He who taught us to pray "Thy will be done" deliver us in order that we might live contrary to that will?

A love that always gives a child what they want, and always withholds what they do not want, is either very short sighted, or does not flow from the heart of a father. So, this consumer-friendly god must be an idol. While we promote a god who loves us, we deny that his love is so intense

---

[174] Deuteronomy 32:21.
[175] Ezekiel 11:11,12.
[176] Hebrews 12:28,29.
[177] Romans 3:18.

that it provokes him to jealousy when we pursue other lovers;[178] rather, we envision a love that allows us to freely chase after them. Those who minimize the seriousness of spiritual adultery, and ignore the reality of jealousy in God on its account, seek nothing less than to eliminate one of the greatest evidences of His love for His people. That love must be very shallow, indeed, which would allow one's spouse to pursue other lovers with little consequence or concern. We reject this side of God not because we exalt love, but because we minimize its intensity and redefine it. But even truth that is obvious will not be seen when one's heart is intensely opposed to it.

The God preached to our customers today sounds very different from the God preached in ages past. Listen to the advice that Joseph Alleine gives to potential customers,

> You are not only without God, but God is against you. Oh, if God would stand neutral that devils should tear and torture him to their utmost power and skill, yet this were not half so fearful. But God will set himself against the sinner (Heb 10:31). There is no friend like Him, no enemy like Him. God Himself will be your tormentor; your destruction shall come from the presence of the Lord (2 Thess 1:9, Rev 6:15-17, Ezek 5:8).[179]

If the idol that we have erected to entice any potential customer does not square with this concept of God, it is not because the Bible fails to clearly reveal this aspect of His nature, but because our depraved nature will not allow us to see it, even when we come across it in the Bible. Our evangelistic sermons sound very different from Edwards "Sinners in the Hand of an Angry God." The god of today is not taken seriously, because, like spoiled children, we have erected a god who takes his children too seriously, and is even willing to be manipulated to secure their affection.

The essence of the consumer mentality is to put man first. So, is it any wonder that a consumer-driven Christianity, which by nature puts

---

[178] James 4:4-5.

[179] Joseph Alleine, An *Alarm to Unconverted Sinners* (London: Religious Tract Society), 85.

the consumer first, would not view things from the Divine perspective that puts the Creator first, and thus rebel against any teaching that would seem to oppose the supremacy of man? Man would naturally serve a god who surrounds him roundabout with his hedge of protection, for this allows man to continue to occupy the place of center. But God's very nature demands that He be made the center. G. S. Faber describes this false religious consumer mentality when he writes,

> It is not sin that they hate, but the wages of sin; it is not
> God that they love, but their own safety.[180]

In contrast to these days of "God in the hands of angry sinners," listen to the God-centered prayer offered up by Ezra, who even in the view of the human tragedy of the destruction of Jerusalem, and the suffering of the Jews taken into captivity, prayed,

> after all that is come upon us for our evil deeds, and
> for our great trespass, seeing that Thou our God hast
> punished us less than our iniquities deserved.[181]

Only those whose eyes have been opened to the Divine glory, could express such a humbling appreciation for the unmerited favors of God, even amid human tragedy. All those whose eyes are opened only to human glory, would grumble at what they could only perceive to be injustice in God for allowing such suffering.

Nor can any abject to God's wrath on the grounds of His mercy. His mercy is impossible without wrath. And besides, His wrath is being treasured up by those who "despise the riches of His goodness, forbearance, and longsuffering."[182] We cannot fully appreciate the words of Paul in Romans 8:31 ("If God be for us who can be against us?"), unless we first accurately comprehend his prior comments in Romans 2:4 – 5 ("the wrath of God is revealed from heaven against all ungodliness and

---

[180] G. S. Faber, *A Practical Treatise on the Ordinary Operations of the Holy Spirit* (New York: Eastburn, Kirk and Co., 1814), 79.
[181] Ezra 9:13.
[182] Romans 2:4,5.

unrighteousness of men,"), or Ephesians 2:3 ("like the rest, we were by nature objects of wrath."). If we downplay this danger, we downplay the deliverance received.

We have weak views of God's wrath, because we have weak views of His holiness. Therefore, we have weak views of the deliverance that Christ came to procure;[183] and this only weakens the gospel. We cannot overthrow the God of the Bible with an idol of all mercy and love, without likewise overthrowing the gospel itself. God does not draw us unto Himself by flattering us with how glorious we are to Him. It is the tendency of the wicked man to flatter himself in his own eyes.[184] But the gospel was not given to flatter man, but to humble him. And unless it humbles, it cannot heal.

The consumer-driven church has propagated a depraved gospel that arrogantly confers on man the power to turn to Christ whenever he so chooses. If this were the case, then the mere power of persuasion would be all that is necessary to convert anyone. But none can turn without the work of the Spirit on the heart producing conviction of sin. Such sorrow for sin does not merely spring from one who has apprehended a sense of danger, but from a faith that apprehends the Person, work and exalted nature of Christ. Man must not only see that he is a sinner, but that his sins rightly deserve eternal damnation. Those who do not see sin as rightly deserving of eternal damnation, do not view God as infinitely deserving of all our heart, soul, mind and strength, and mistake the very essence of sin. All who do not see God as deserving of all our heart, and this includes both the legalist and the antinomian, have no basis for genuine conviction of sin, because they fail to recognize the very essence of sin, so that all their concern about sin is for its effects on themselves. Such an anti-consumer vision cannot be conjured up at any moment by man, but is possible only by those whose eyes are removed from their self-importance to behold the alluring brightness of His glory. Unless Christ is revealed to the soul by the Spirit, our counterfeit faith will embrace a less glorious counterfeit christ. A person's view of Christ is of the utmost importance in Christianity, not only because all those whom Christ does not so draw by "the brightness

---

[183] Luke 4:18.
[184] Psalms 36:1,2.

47

of His glory"[185] He "shall destroy with the brightness of His coming,"[186] but primarily because this destruction involves being eternally deprived of Him who alone is satisfyingly glorious.[187] He is not glorious because He satisfies, but satisfies some and will terrify others, because He is glorious.

Failure to fulfill the chief end of man (to glorify God for who He is, and to return thanks for what He does),[188] must meet with the direst consequences – the revelation of God's wrath.[189] This wrath is an essential display of God's glory and holiness. All who seek God's glory, and love holiness, will rejoice in this display of holiness as it punishes men for their sins and ultimately sets all things right.[190] To be appalled by this aspect of God's nature is to render more glory to the creature than the Creator. The concept of wrath stresses the seriousness of sin and its total contrariness to God's nature. Take away judgment and the gravity of sin is lost. "He that hath slight thoughts of sin had never great thoughts of God,"[191] says Owen. Therefore, those who prefer a god of all love, prefer a god who is indifferent to sin, and therefore stripped of his gloriousness. Only those who do not see sin as grievous, nor God as glorious, would wish that it had no consequences. We will never glorify God as God, unless we are granted correct views of His glorious nature. Those who are blind to the brightness of His glory, will entertain many perplexing difficulties concerning the reality hell and God's present dealings with man in judgment and providence. Universalism is only an attractive counterfeit offer for those who are blind to Christ's glory and beauty. And its acceptance, like all counterfeit offers, is itself the result of God's judgment in abandoning men to their erroneous views of both Himself and themselves.

One part of God's present judgment is to deprive men of Himself by abandoning a people to the consequences of their sins:

---

[185] Hebrews 1:3.

[186] 2 Thessalonians 2:8.

[187] 2 Thessalonians 2:9.

[188] Romans 1:21.

[189] Romans 1:18.

[190] Psalm 96:11 – 13.

[191] John Owen, *The Works of John Owen D. D. Vol. VI* (London and Edinburgh: Johnstone and Hunter, 1851), 394.

God also gave them up.[192]

God gave them over to a debased mind, to do those things which are not fitting.[193]

God will send them strong delusions, that they should believe the lie, that they all may be condemned who did not believe the truth but had pleasure in unrighteousness.[194]

So I gave them up unto their own hearts' lust: and they walked in their own counsels.[195]

Then God turned, and gave them up to worship the host of heaven.[196]

We would be mistaken to view God as merely passive in these verses. Commenting on these verses, P. T. Forsyth asks several poignant questions,

> Is it enough to say that this is but the actions of a process which God simply watches in a permissive way? Is He but passive and not positive to the situation? Can the Absolute be passive to anything?[197]

Leon Morris also writes,

> In these very verses, we find the personal activity of God brought out, for when St. Paul might well say that the sins of the heathen produced inevitable results, or might make use of some similar expression, he seems to

---

[192] Romans 1:24,26.

[193] Romans 1:28

[194] 2 Thessalonians 2:11,12.

[195] Psalms 81: 12.

[196] Acts 7:42.

[197] P. T. Forsyth, *Christianity According to St. Paul* (Cambridge, 1927), 78.

go out of his way to lay stress upon the divine activity. God gave them up.[198]

In this life, the greatest judgment is to be left in our own rebellion against Him. To be given up to our own preferences is not only a dangerous prospect, but a dangerous philosophy of ministry. "There is no greater punishment," says Pasquier Quesnel, "than that of being abandoned to one's self."[199] Many fear the greatest evil in the removal of their power, wealth and so-called wisdom. But for many, the real evil is not the removal, but the continuance of all these things.[200] Thomas Brooks said,

> God doth plague and punish them most with spiritual judgments – which are the greatest, the sorest and heaviest – whom He least punishes with temporal punishments.[201]

The greatest judgment of God is to be left to continue unhindered down the path of degradation; experiencing the consequences of such a negative life-style in the present life, while still treasuring up wrath for the day of wrath which is to come.

> Whene'er becalm'd I lie,
> And storms forbear to toss;
> Be Thou, dear Lord, still nigh,
> Lest I should suffer loss:
> For more the treacherous calm I dread,
> Than tempests bursting o'er my head.

---

[198] Leon Morris, *The Apostolic Preaching of the Cross* (Grand Rapids: Eerdmans Publishing Company, 1956), 166.

[199] Pasquier Quesnel, from *Christian Pioneer* Vol XXIX (London: Simpkin, Marshall & CO, 1875), 47.

[200] See Edwards sermon entitled "*Those Whom God Hates, He Often Gives plenty of Earthly Things To.*" From *Knowing the Heart*: Jonathan Edwards on True and False Conversion (Ames: International Outreach, 2003), 125.

[201] Thomas Brooks, *The Complete Works of Thomas Brooks,* Vol. I (Edinburgh: James Nichol, 1866), 45.

Than tempests bursting o'er my head."[202]

Being part of the visible people of God does not exempt one from God's judgment, for judgment must begin at the house of God.[203] "It is a fearful thing to fall into the hands of the living God,"[204] is prefaced by "The Lord shall judge His people." John Owen writes,

> The rule of His continuance with any people or church, as to the outward dispensation of His providence and the means of grace, is that expressed in 2 Chron. xv. 2, 'The Lord is with you, while ye be with Him; and if ye seek Him, He will be found of you; but if ye forsake Him, He will forsake you.' He judicially forsakes them by whom He is willfully forsaken.[205]

The prophet Jeremiah warns,

> Shall I not, as I have done unto Samaria and her idols, so do to Jerusalem and her idols.[206]

Sinners in Zion are in a very fearful state, because the false assurance that they constantly receive desensitizes them to the gospel. The fact that they are continually affirmed, and the warning of Isaiah is rarely heard, renders the situation all the direr. "The sinners in Zion are afraid; fearfulness hath surprised the hypocrites. Who among us shall dwell with the devouring fire? Who among us shall dwell with everlasting burnings?"[207] The false confidence gained by many from being part of the visible church is no more justifiable than the argument of the Jews that simply having Abraham for their father secured them a place in God's

---

[202] John Stanford, *The Domestic Chaplain* (London: John Bennett, 1825), 109.

[203] 1 Peter 4:17,18.

[204] Hebrews 10:30,31.

[205] John Owen, *The Works of John Owen, D. D.* Vol. VII (London and Edinburgh: Johnstone and Hunter, 1852), 141.

[206] Isaiah 10:11.

[207] Isaiah 33:14.

Kingdom.[208] What Paul said concerning circumcision can easily apply to the rites and privileges of the church.

> For he is not a Jew, which is one outwardly, neither is that circumcision, which is outward in the flesh: But he is a Jew, which is one inwardly, and circumcision is that of the heart, in the spirit, and not in the letter; whose praise is not of men, but of God.[209]

Although its purpose is not unto condemnation, but salvation, even true believers are not exempt from God's judgment. "But when we are judged, we are chastened of the Lord, that we should not be condemned with the world."[210] If God so hates sin that He must chasten His own people to the increase of their obedience,[211] what a fearful state and what awful judgment must await those, even within the visible church, who are left without this chastening for the confirmation of their disobedience? "God shall send them strong delusion, that they should believe a lie.... who believe not the truth, but had pleasure in unrighteousness."[212]

The great apostasy that Paul referred to in 2 Thessalonians 2 and 2 Timothy 3 are to take place within the church. They involve those who have "a form of godliness, but denying the power thereof."[213] There will always be men within the church who "serve not our Lord Jesus Christ, but their own belly; and by good words and fair speeches deceive the hearts of the simple."[214] They will handle the word of God deceitfully.[215] And, like the Jews of Isaiah's day, there will be those who engage in much religious activity, but still choose their own ways.[216] God responds to this rejection the same way today – "I also will choose their delusion."[217] And the reason

---

[208] Matthew 3:7 – 10.

[209] Romans 2:28,29.

[210] 1 Corinthians 11:32.

[211] Revelations 3:19; Hosea 5:15.

[212] 2 Thessalonians 2:11,12.

[213] 2 Timothy 3:5; see also 2 Corinthians 11:13,14.

[214] Romans 16:18.

[215] 2 Corinthians 4:2.

[216] Isaiah 66:3.

[217] Isaiah 66:4a.

given is the same – "because when I called, none did answer; when I spake, they did not hear; but they did evil before mine eyes, and chose that in which I delighted not."[218]

God sends this delusion by withholding His grace, thereby allowing men to believe a lie, so that they pursue unrighteousness even within the visible church. Their own wickedness will be their punishment.[219] When men do not tremble at God's word,[220] God will choose for them a delusion that will confirm them in their disobedience. When we become consumer-driven, we will grant the people's request – "Prophesy not unto us right things, but speak unto us smooth things, prophesy deceits."[221] We do not love holiness; therefore, we invent theologies that allow us the option of eliminating its necessity.[222] When men take pleasure in unrighteousness, they will maintain the form of righteousness, but embrace theologies that allow them to deny its power, or excuse their unrighteousness.

Dispensationalism is one of the theologies that is especially designed to deny the power of godliness, while encouraging the form. While it correctly waits for a future Kingdom, it minimizes a present Kingdom that must be pressed into now. It is not by chance that most of the verses that exhort us to "be not deceived,"[223] refer to being deceived in believing that believers have the option of including disobedience and unrighteousness into their lifestyle with no eternal consequences. Dispensationalism is a delusion that affords some of its customers the luxury of being counted Christians, and entitled to heaven, while still enjoying a lifestyle characterized by unrighteousness. They believe in a power of godliness that is optional for all believers, and much of their efforts in theology is in proving this erroneous teaching. While they maintain that works are very desirable, they do not believe that they are necessary for the existence of genuine saving faith. Their attempt to elevate justification through faith, by lowing the fruit and characteristic of the faith that justifies, ruins the doctrine altogether, and affirms that it is possible to be justified by a dead

---

[218] Isaiah 66:4b.

[219] Jeremiah 2:19.

[220] Isaiah 66:2.

[221] Isaiah 30:10.

[222] Ephesians 4:22; Titus 3:3; 2 Timothy 4:3.

[223] 1 John 3:7; Ephesians 5:5-8; 1 Corinthians 6:9 – 11, 15:33 – 34, Galatians 5:21, 6:7 – 8.

faith that doesn't work. And this is done not for the fear of the opposite extreme of legalism, for even in Galatians, where Paul confronts legalism, this same warning against antinomianism appears. Like Paul, we must confront legalism and antinomianism together. Those who can only bring themselves to oppose one of these, are only promoting the other. Those who turn the grace of God into lasciviousness,[224] will always attract those who do not desire to flee from unrighteousness, but merely from the horrors of hell. And if we do not have a heart to obey God, He will permit us to choose any number of delusions that exist in today's ecclesiastical marketplace that will allow us to choose our own ways, while still believing ourselves to be His followers on our way to heaven.

Consumer-driven Christianity is not the cause of God's judgments, it is God's righteous judgment upon those who choose the creature over the Creator in religion. As some are set upon embracing idolatrous lies, God withholds His true prophets, and even allows false prophets among His professed people, to test the reality of their love for Him and His truth, and thus confirm them in their lie. "Thou shall not hearken unto the words of that prophet, or that dreamer of dreams: for the Lord your God proveth you, to know whether ye love the Lord your God with all your heart and with all your soul."[225] God's judgment in this case is righteous, for those who fall prey to such prophets do so "after their own lusts."[226] The exposing of false prophets, although the apparent judgment of God upon the false prophet, (so that "they shall proceed no further"),[227] is an act of mercy upon the people of God. Whenever they are espoused by the professed people of God, and permitted to continue unhindered in the church, it is a sign of His judgment.

Karl Barth, who followed many of his own created delusions, both theological and practical, succeeded in hitting the nail on head when he wrote,

> The forgetting of the God is already itself the breaking loose of His wrath against those who forget Him (i, 18).

---

[224] Jude 4.
[225] Deuteronomy 13:1 – 4.
[226] 2 Timothy 4:3.
[227] 2 Timothy 3:9.

> The enterprise of setting up the 'no-God' is avenged
> with success.......when God has been deprived of His
> glory, men are deprived of theirs.[228]

The consumer-driven church, by following the false god of the masses, has only encouraged the no-god philosophy of the heathen of Romans 1 and 2, which in turn receives the same judgment of God upon it in the form of an ethical crisis. "Who knowing the judgment of God, that they which commit such things are worthy of death, not only do the same, but have pleasure in them that do them."[229]

Practical atheism and doctrinal atheism have the same cause and effect. For that reason, the Puritans were not only the most practical theologians, but, because of this practicality, were the most consistently logical theologians. If both doctrine and practice are equally conducive to the glory of God, then those who do not equally promote both sides of theology, will find themselves opposing the glory of God. The apparent success of the consumer-driven church within a consumer society is not an evidence of divine favor, but proof of divine judgment, as God merely gives them what they want.[230] For when Christianity is hijacked by the consumer, it is not a sign that judgment is impending, but that "the glory," has already "departed."[231]

---

[228] Karl Barth, *The Epistle of the Romans* (London: Oxford University Press, 1968; original 1933), 51.

[229] Romans 2:32.

[230] "Then, therefore, does God give up men to delusions, when in His providence He affords such advantages unto them by whom they are to be deluded; for those who possess the place of outward veneration may lead a backsliding multitude unto what they please." Owen, *Works* Vol. VII, 143, 144.

[231] 1 Samuel 4:21.

CHAPTER 6

Wide Is The Gate, The Allure Of Consumer-Driven Christianity

> Enter ye in at the straight gate, for wide is the gate, and
> broad is the way, that leadeth to destruction, and many
> there be which go in thereat.
>
> Matthew 7:13

The primary problem with consumer-driven Christianity is its misplaced trust. Faith is that which ultimately distinguishes the city of God from the city of man. Man looks to himself and depends upon himself for all he seeks. The consumer-driven church unites against God with the city of man in that which is most displeasing to God – unbelief. While the acts of unbelief may not always be outwardly evil, they are evil, nonetheless, in their misguided trust. Even in things neutral, the act may be evil if the underlying principle is wicked. Lack of faith may prompt many to pursue the good of the church through their own means, and this lack of trust in the One who is the head of the church renders their efforts evil in His sight. To follow the narrow way, one must embrace the ethics of the Kingdom. The principles of action that flow only from belief in a god who is a far off, will promote the fleshly principles of trusting to our own devices, and lead us to indulge the flesh through compromise. For when we imitate the principles of a society without faith, we must inevitably follow it to its only logical application – "Let us eat and drink; for to-morrow we die."[232]

The church cannot depend on the marketing principles of the world for its growth without likewise sharing in the shallowness that is the necessary result of reaching such a vast and diverse audience without offending any potential customer. And its constant evolution into newer and more exciting forms of expression, which allows it to compete for the attention of those in the marketplace, brings it ever closer to the spirit of the world from which these principles spring. The consequence of consumer-driven Christianity, then, becomes the present judgment of God upon it, as it is given over by God to the spirit of the world to experience the same emptiness, shallowness and degeneration of the marketplace. Consumer-driven Christianity, by rejecting Christianity's historical center for the shifting preferences of its modern customers, is worldliness, and all worldliness has its consequences. And the results are described by the apostle Paul,

> Because they received not the love of the truth, that they might be saved. And for this cause God shall send them strong delusion, that they should believe a lie: that they all might be damned who believe not the truth, but had pleasure in unrighteousness.[233]

The Bible is full of examples of those who desired to invent their own religion while opposing the true worship of God. And nowhere are the subsequent evil consequences more readily seen than in the book of Judges. When "every man did that which was right in his own eyes,"[234] the end was tragic. Such tragedy does not always manifest itself in the loss of outer vitality in the church. It is possible for a church to have a name that they live, and yet be dead.[235] And there is no greater sign of spiritual death, then when the church is characterized by the spirit of those who do that which is right in their own eyes. And like successful celebrities, when

---

[232] 1 Corinthians 15:32.
[233] 2 Thessalonians 2:10 – 12.
[234] Judges 21:25.
[235] Revelation 3:1.

every church is free to reinvent Christianity into whatever form they desire, the more singular, unique or creative they can be, the more attention they gain for themselves.

Gregory Bedell describes the ethics of consumer-driven Christianity as those "who hope to find the essence of Christianity between the extremes of hot and cold." Listen as he describes this lukewarm condition:

> They dare not, for fear of hell, give themselves altogether to the world, and they will not, for love of the world, give themselves wholly to Christ; and they thus vacillate between the two, sometimes a little inclining to the one, and sometimes to the other; afraid to be either, hoping to be both; desirous of being the friend of God and a friend of the world. Lukewarmness, is a kind of vain idea that religion is something in which we cannot heartily concur, and yet which we do not like altogether to lose.[236]

For fear of the punishment of hell or hopes of the happiness of heaven, the selfishness of many church-goers will not allow them to lose religion altogether. What is it that dictates the ethics and guides the actions of consumer-driven Christianity? Self-preservation – "I don't want to go to hell," and self-indulgence – "but I don't want to miss out on earth either." They can rejoice that their sins are forgiven (past, present and future), only because they are indifferent whether their future communion with God is affected or not. One cannot presently rejoice over the future forgiveness of any sin that may affect his future fellowship, unless he is a mere religious consumer who cares only for the benefits of his relationship with God, and nothing for God Himself.

Those who are reconciled, however, have a different value system from those of the world. They cannot rejoice merely in a name to live. The greatest loss for them is not the loss of any attention or notoriety, but the very absence of God's presence in their lives or ministry. The far heavier judgment is when God says,

---

[236] Gregory Bedell, *Sermons by rev. Gregory T. Bedell, D.D.*, Vol. II (Philadelphia: William Stavely – John C. Pechin, 1835), 397.

> I will go and return to My place, till they acknowledge
> their offence, and seek My face: in their affliction, they
> will seek Me early."[237]

He teaches them the goodness of His presence, by the evilness of His absence. Seeing the value of what was lost should bring about a closer and more careful walk with Him. But we do not feel the weightiness of this loss, because we do not see the value of His presence. Listen how Robert Leighton describes the blessedness of this presence:

> Though we all profess to know God, yet, the greatest
> part of us are so far from duly esteeming Him, that we
> do not at all know what the spiritual, gracious presence
> of God is; how sweet the enjoyment, and how bitter and
> sad the deprivement. Oh, be desirous to understand and
> know this highest good, and, above all things, seek to
> enjoy it! And without doubt, the experience of it will
> persuade you to prize it and entertain it carefully; never
> willing to grieve and drive away so great and so good a
> Guest, who brings true happiness along with Him to
> those with whom He dwells.[238]

The greatest tragedy is when we, like Samson,[239] fail to recognize, until it is too late, that the presence of the Spirit is already gone.

The sentiment of all those who love God supremely is: "Let goods and kindred go, this mortal life also." The sentiment of many today, however, is: "We have secured God and a place in heaven, now let us secure, with God's help, a place on earth as well." They only seek God early, who have ceased to seek themselves in their search for Him. This the consumer will never do, because he seeks things for the benefits they render to self, and not for the intrinsic value of the thing sought. Ultimately, God is the highest good. But the consumer cannot see this, because he values

---

[237] Hosea 5:15.

[238] Robert Leighton, *The Whole Works of the Most Revered Father in God, Robert Leighton, D.D.*, Vol. II (London: Henry G. Bohn, 1846), 413.

[239] Judges 16:20.

himself too highly. To obtain this ultimate good, man must become anti-consumer; in other words, he must be found before he will seek. "He that loveth his life shall lose it; and he that hateth his life in this world shall keep it unto life eternal."[240]

God purposely put an offence in the message of the cross to render it unattractive to self. As a result, those who would seek Him and find Him cannot do so under the power of self, nor from the primary motive of self. Real Christianity is foolish from the world's point of view; "If in this life only we have hope in Christ, we are of all men most miserable."[241] Paul concludes that, from the world's perspective, we lose in this life. But doesn't Hebrews 11:6 tell us that "he that cometh to God must believe that He is, and that He is a rewarder of them that diligently seek Him?" Yes, but many of the heroes of faith in that chapter do not look like they were rewarded, unless we have an erroneous view of rewards! Upon a closer examination, it becomes obvious that the rewards experienced by these people were of another nature than those commonly sought after by the world or offered by the church.

When we tell the lost that "God loves them and has a wonderful plan for their lives," we must be very clear as to what that plan might entail. If we mean wonderful from the world's point of view, we not only give false expectations, but also encourage them to seek themselves in religion. Ultimately God's plan for all of these heroes of faith was wonderful, but before they could arrive at their reward some had to travel the path of "trial of cruel mockings and scourgings, yea, moreover of bonds and imprisonments: they were stoned, they were sawn asunder, were tempted, were slain with sword: they wandered about in sheepskins and goatskins; being destitute, afflicted, tormented."[242] In essence, the way of faith that leads to rewards always directs its travelers down paths of self-denial and self-sacrifice, rather than self-indulgence.

It is not selfish to have "respect unto the recompense of reward,"[243] so long as the recompense of reward is rightly defined. Even Christ sets forth rewards in His beatitudes with such statements as:

---

[240] John 12:25.
[241] 1 Corinthians 15:19.
[242] Hebrews 11:36,37
[243] Hebrews 11:26

theirs is the Kingdom of heaven,

they shall inherit the earth,

they shall see God,

they shall be called children of God,

great is your reward in heaven.[244]

Such rewards are not only lawful, but they become our duty to seek and expect. For the same grace that is "teaching us that, denying ungodliness and worldly lust, we should live soberly, righteously, and godly, in this present world,"[245] also teaches us to "look for that blessed hope, and the glorious appearing of the great God and our Saviour Jesus Christ."[246] These rewards are Christ-centered. Certainly, the offers of success, wealth or the gratification of felt-needs is inconsistent with the hopes of those who earnestly desire His appearing.

While the rewards offered by consumer-driven Christianity may be compatible with man in either his unregenerate or regenerate state, the beatitudes point to other rewards that can be enjoyed by none but the spiritual minded. Man, regenerate and unregenerate alike, may enjoy creation and material things, but the regenerate only values those things as secondary, which the unregenerate values as primary. In this, the city of man within the city of God, will always show its true colors. Enjoy these things we may, but he who seeks true riches will not be too anxious to acquire those things that the Gentiles seek. He will rather be ready to sacrifice them all, if necessary, to gain that which faith seeks above them all. The values of the city of man may mimic for its our advantage those of the city of God, but without true faith, these values cannot be welcome in the heart.

It is perfectly legitimate to have respect unto the recompense of reward to encourage self-sacrifice in the service of God, just as it did in the life

---

[244] Matthew 5:3-12
[245] Titus 2:12
[246] Tutus 2:13

of Moses, the other heroes of faith, and even Christ Himself.[247] But that legitimacy depends entirely on how one first defines and then follows the recompense of reward. The joy that was set before Christ was not selfish, but for the resulting redemption of man and the pleasure of the Father. The prophet Isaiah writes,

> Yet it pleased the Father to bruise Him; He has put Him to grief: when Thou shalt make His soul an offering for sin, He shall see His seed, He shall prolong His days, and the pleasure of the Lord shall prosper in His hand. He shall see the travail of His soul, and shall be satisfied: by His knowledge shall My Righteous Servant justify many; for He shall bear their iniquities.[248]

Concerning this Jonathan Edwards writes,

> This implies that Christ has His delight, most truly and properly, in obtaining the salvation of His church, not merely as a means conducing to the thing which terminate His delight and joy; but as what He rejoices and is satisfied in, most directly and properly.[249]

If Moses esteemed the reproach of Christ greater riches than the treasures of Egypt, for he had respect unto the recompense of the reward,[250] then certainly the reward that he looked to must have been esteemed far greater than all the earthly riches, position and authority that he laid aside in order to pursue it, and not merely an alternative route by which they might be obtained. Likewise, we do not rejoice and delight in God's glory as a means to advance our own joy and happiness, but as it is in itself our very happiness. God is a rewarded of those who diligently seek Him, and not of those who diligently seek ways to use Him. Since God is

---

[247] Hebrews 12:2.

[248] Isaiah 53:10 – 11.

[249] Jonathan Edwards, *The Works of President Edwards*, Vol. II (New York: Leavitt, Trow, & CO, 1844), 243.

[250] Hebrews 11:26.

ultimately the greatest joy of His people, our greatest reward must consist in that which is His greatest delight – His own glory and communicating this glory to His creatures. Simply because our greatest happiness comes from pursuing the ultimate end, does not imply that our happiness is our ultimate end. The ultimate end, if it is indeed the ultimate end, can only be sought for its own sake. Our reward will be happiness, only because God, not happiness, is our portion. It was possible for Christ to face the destiny of the cross with joy, only because the work of redemption had God's glory as its highest and ultimate end.

Do we look for a city whose builder and maker is God?[251] If not, then we cannot expect to persevere long in our Christian journey, for we have not yet even commenced our journey toward Him, but still pursue self. John Bunyan, in the Pilgrim's Progress, mentions four companions who were on their way toward the celestial city; Mr. Hold-the-world, Mr. Money-love, Mr. Save-all and Mr. By-ends. These men "were taught by one Mr. Gripe-man, a schoolmaster in Love-gain, which is a market-town in the country of Coveting, in the north. This schoolmaster taught them the art of getting, either by violence, cozenage, flattery, lying, or by putting on the guise of religion."[252] Christian tells these men,

> if it be unlawful to follow Christ for the loaves, as it is, (John vi) how much more is it abominable to make of Him and religion a stalking-horse, to get and enjoy the world? The man that takes up religion for the world, will throw away religion for the world.

Despite all of the many biblical examples that Christian could muster, it is difficult to dissuade most men from those false principles taught in the market-town of Love-gain once they have taken up religion upon this false pretext and have so many companions who think as they do. Therefore, those who embrace a Christianity tailored to their fallen desires, will hardly heed the biblical warnings of a few lonely pilgrims.

Our religion should dictate our practice in the marketplace. But

---

[251] Hebrews 11:10.

[252] John Bunyan, *The Complete Works of John Bunyan* (Philadelphia: Bradley, Garretson and Co., 1873), 138 – 141.

once the marketplace dictates the practice of our religion, which is the very essence of consumer-driven Christianity, it is spiritually fatal. These men, at the first invitation of Demas, were turned aside to his silver mine. Bunyan stresses their tragic outcome,

> Now whether they fell into the pit by looking over the brink thereof, or whether they went down to dig, or whether they were smothered in the bottom by the damps that commonly arise, of these things I am not certain; but this I observed, that they never were seen again in the way.

All those who take up Christianity as a business deal to advance some selfish end, are equally in danger of being turned aside into every false path where their selfish heart will take them. While they may remain physically within the church, and even prosper in ministry therein, they have long since abandoned the pilgrimage. Christ cannot be followed with ulterior motives. Unless our selfish heart is changed, we are not on the narrow path that leads to life.[253] The Word becomes unproductive when it is choked out by the cares of the world or the deceitfulness of riches.[254]

All the warnings given to the individual believer can equally apply to the church corporately, especially since the church is only a reflection of its individual members. Therefore, what does it profit the church, if it shall gain the whole world, while in the process lose its very soul?[255] When the essence of Christianity is lost, the increase in numbers do not justify the techniques, but further expands the tragedy. "If the blind lead the blind, both shall fall into the ditch."[256]

> "Thus, the most are carried with the stream of this wicked world, their own inward corruption easily agreeing and suiting with it; every man, as a drop, falling

---

[253] Matthew 7:13 - 14.
[254] Matthew 13:22.
[255] Matthew 16:26.
[256] Matthew 15:14.

into a torrent, and easily made one, and running along
with it into that dead sea where it empties itself."[257]

Robert Leighton

True Christianity is contrary to the world in that it must arrive at its
destination by traveling upstream, rather than by striving to keep up with
the multitude rushing downward towards destruction. To accommodate
the church to the masses is to lead her through the wide gate. For the
wide gate is always revealed by the path of the majority. And, as Charles
Drelincourt rightly observed,

> It is not possible to go to heaven by treading the paths
> of hell.[258]

To lead men on the wide path under the guise of compassion, is
deception. The difference between a zeal for souls and a zeal to merely
gather disciples after ourselves for our own glory, is the call to discipleship.
Those who desire to honor Christ will call men to allegiance to Him;
therefore, if disciples are not being made, the preeminence of Christ is
not in view, and the church itself becomes the wide gate that leads to
destruction – the promoter of nominal Christianity.

---

[257] Leighton. *Works,* Vol. I, 370.
[258] Charles Drelincourt, *The Christian's Defense Against the Fears of Death,
with Seasonable Directions how to Die Well* (London: Thomas Kelly, 1814), 167.

PART II

DELIVERANCE:

Allured by the Brightness of His glory

"The first work, which God put forth upon the soul, in order to its conversion, is to raise up a spiritual light within it, to clear up its apprehensions about spiritual matters, so as to enable the soul to look upon God as the chiefest good, and the enjoyment of Him as the greatest bliss….Where God intends to work over a soul to Himself, He doth not only pass an enlightening act upon the understanding and its apprehensions, but likewise a sanctifying act upon the will and its affections, that when the soul perceives the glory of God, and the beauty of holiness, it may presently close with, and entertain it with the choicest of its affections. And without God's thus drawing it, the understanding could never allure the soul to good."[259]

William Beveridge

---

[259] William Beveridge, *Private Thoughts on Religion and a Christian Life* (Philadelphia: Thomas Kite, 1829), 66,67.

CHAPTER 7

Deliverance from Sin and Wrath

Who gave Himself for our sins, that He might deliver
us from this present evil world.

Galatians 1:4

Even Jesus, which delivered us from the wrath to come.

1 Thessalonians 1:10

Salvation is defined as that by which we draw near unto God and are
delivered from that which separates us from Him. Since relationship
to God is central in salvation, and sin affects that relationship, the work of
Christ must propitiate God by expiating our sins and removing them from
His sight. Justification is necessary to restore our favor and friendship. "And
you, that were sometime alienated and enemies in your mind by wicked
works, yet now hath He reconciled in the body of His flesh through death,
to present you holy, and unblameable, and unreproveable in His sight."[260]

Because man is so impotent, and sin so serious, deliverance requires
a serious solution – the sacrifice of God's own Son on the cross. And one
must suppose that such an extraordinary sacrifice must effect the most
amazing cure. Not a partial cure that includes merely the forgiveness of
our past sinful behavior, the removal of the law's curse and declaring us
righteous in justification, but a total cure that includes the breaking of sin's
reigning power over the soul in regeneration, the securing of our future

---

[260] Colossians 1:21,22.

walk of holiness in sanctification, and ultimately that experience of total separation from the presence of sin whereby we stand before Him perfected in glorification. For we are not only saved by His death, but also by His life. Being reconciled, we shall be saved by His life.[261] God not only "sent His Son to be the propitiation for our sins,"[262]

> God sent His only begotten Son into the world, that we might live through Him.[263]

> Who His own self bare our sins in His own body on the tree, that we, being dead to sins, should live unto righteousness: by whose stripes ye were healed.[264]

> And that He died for all, that they which live should not henceforth live unto themselves, but unto Him which died for them, and rose again.[265]

Unless our concept of deliverance includes all these, it can only be a deliverance marketed to suit the preferences of the customer over the eternal purposes of God.

Deliverance that is marketed towards the consumer will disproportionately address those aspects of deliverance that most benefit the consumer, rather than those aspects of the work of God in the soul that most glorify Him. Forgiveness is not the end in our salvation. While it is true that "God so loved the world that He gave His only begotten Son, that whosoever believeth in Him should not perish, but have everlasting life,"[266] Christ more narrowly defined this life when He said, "this is eternal life, that they might know Thee."[267] This spiritual knowledge does not only accompany spiritual life, it is also the ultimate end of eternal life. Such a life aspires toward the further knowledge of Him and His glory, and not

---

[261] Romans 5:10.

[262] 1 John 4:10.

[263] 1 John 4:9.

[264] 1 Peter 2:24.

[265] 2 Corinthians 5:15.

[266] John 3:16.

[267] John 17:3.

in the fulfillment of our list of consumer preferences. If it is merely the forgiveness of sin that we want, then we have not the least idea of what sin is. It is from the habitual practice of always asking ourselves, "What's in it for me?" that we need forgiveness. While we may all confess that we are sinners, if we do not desire a new heart, our confession only mocks God.

The gospel "is the power of God unto salvation to every one that believeth."[268] If this salvation is defined solely as justification, forgiveness and adoption, then the only power that God exerts in salvation is toward Himself in declaring the sinner righteous and bestowing upon him the benefit of adoption. The gospel does not issue forth in an objective power alone, but also subjectively in the new birth. God exercises His creative power in the gospel both by imputing and imparting His righteousness, and by bestowing both the title and the nature of sons. Listen as Edward Polhill totally discredits those who would market salvation in a more narrowly defined form, which picks and chooses those benefits that are perceived as most beneficial to self, while refusing or ignoring those by which self is conquered,

Did God exact so great a satisfaction for sin, that it might be allowed? Did He vindicate His broken law at so high a rate, that it might be more broken, and that with impunity? It is utterly impossible; those sufferings of Christ which did witness God's hatred of sin, could not open a gap to it; the Surety did not sweat, pray, bleed, and die under wrath, that the impenitent sinner might be spared. O how profane and blasphemous is such a thought, which makes the great Redeemer a patron of iniquity! He came to save us from our sins, not in them; to redeem from iniquity, not to encourage it.[269]

Listen also as Jonathan Edwards describes the utter contrariness of such persons with the saving purposes of God,

> Such persons as these, instead of embracing Christ as
> their Saviour from sin, trust in Him as the Saviour of
> their sins; instead of flying to Him as their refuge from
> spiritual enemies, they make use of Him as the defense

---

[268] Romans 1:16.

[269] Edward Polhill, *A View of Some Divine Truths* (London: A. M. and R. R. for Tho. Cockerill, 1678), 68.

of their spiritual enemies, from God, and to strengthen them against Him. They make Christ the minister of sin, and great officer and vicegerent of the devil, to strengthen his interest, and make him above all things in the world strong against Jehovah; so that they may sin against Him with good courage, and without fear, being effectually secured from restraints, by His most solemn warnings and most awful threatenings.[270]

And finally, hear J. C. Ryle affirm the same,

Many would like much to escape the punishment of sin, who will not strive to be free from its power; they wish to be justified but not sanctified; they desire much to have God's favour, but they care little for God's image and likeness; their talk is of pardon, but not of purity; they think much about God's willingness to forgive, but little about His warning that we be renewed. But this is leaving out of sight half the work which Christ died to perform: He died that we might become holy as well as happy, He purchased grace to sanctify as well as grace to redeem; and now forgiveness of sin and change of heart must never be separated.[271]

Deliverance from Wrath: A 2-Fold Reconciliation

The gospel cannot clearly reveal who Christ is and what He has done, without also discovering the hostility that exist between God and man. Unless this hostility is clearly seen, the real nature of both God and man have not yet been sufficiently unveiled, and therefore the work of Christ cannot be properly understood, nor His Person fully embraced. Without this saving knowledge of Christ, we will attempt to persuade men to

---

[270] Jonathan Edwards, *The Works of President Edwards*, Vol. III (New York: Leavitt, Trow, & CO, 1844), 168.
[271] J C Ryle, The True Christian (Grand Rapids: Baker Book House, 1978; original 1900), 53.

receive the benefits of Christ's death without urging them on Christ's behalf to be reconciled to God[272] as the greatest benefit of His death and highest manifestation of Christ's love.[273]

It is because of the hostility that exists between God and man, and not merely for the lesser consequences of our sin that Christ came. Redemption has a higher purpose in the plan of God than merely helping man out of all his troubles. It finds its central purpose in Christ, and has a uniting affect to Him in both union and communion.[274] Once the hostility has been removed, these other consequences are resolved. The greater includes the lesser.[275] Isaiah summarizes man's primary problem,

> the Lord's hand is not shortened, that it cannot save: neither His ear heavy, that it cannot hear: but your iniquities have separated between you and your God, and your sins have hid His face from you, that He will not hear.[276]

The work of reconciliation is possible only through the means of a mediator. "For there is one God, and one mediator between God and men, the man Christ Jesus."[277] A mediator is one who intervenes between two parties to reconcile them. Reconciliation with God must take into account all of His attributes. Those who view God as all mercy and love, without holiness and justice, will see no need for reconciliation. Those who see Him as all holiness and justice, without mercy and love, will see no possibility of reconciliation.

Reconciliation must also consider all of man's present condition. The necessity of Christ's sacrifice lies both in the nature of God and the nature of man. God could not simply forgive man's sins and befriend him, because He cannot cease to be Himself, a just and holy God who hates sin. Nor could man, under his own power, lay down his arms and turn from his sins, because he also cannot cease to be what he is, a rebellious sinner.

---

[272] 2 Corinthians 5:20.
[273] 1 John 3:1.
[274] Ephesians 1:9,10.
[275] Romans 8:31,32.
[276] Isaiah 59:1,2.
[277] 1 Timothy 2:5.

To remove this hostility, a change must take place in both the relationship of God to man, and man to God. Leon Morris confirms the necessity of a two-fold reconciliation when he writes,

> We maintain, therefore, that there is no good reason for rejecting the conclusion to which the biblical evidence points, namely, that reconciliation includes what we must call a change on the part of God as well as on the part of man, since the wrath of God is no longer directed towards man.[278]

The gospel does not change the nature of God. Christ did not have to die in order for God to love the sinner, but only to render the exercise of His love consistent with His own justice.[279] Samuel Rutherford says,

> Reconciliation turneth not the heart, but the hand of the Lord upon the little ones, as He speaketh, so that he cannot deal with or punish His elect, as otherwise He would do.[280]

Although Christ is "the Lamb slain from the foundation of the world,"[281] this does not imply that man is justified or reconciled from eternity any more than the world, which was also part of God's eternal plan, was created from eternity. Until man believes, he remains under the wrath of God. "He that believeth not is condemned already."[282] "And were by nature the children of wrath, even as others."[283] What God has purposed from all eternity, must take place in space and time to become reality.

"God is always willing and ready to be reconciled with His enemies,"

---

[278] Leon Morris, *The Apostolic Preaching of the Cross* (Grand Rapids: Eerdmans Publishing Company, 1956), 222,223.

[279] John 3:16, Romans 3:25,26.

[280] Samuel Rutherford, *The Trial and Triumph of Faith* (Choteau: Old Paths Gospel Press, reprint), 367.

[281] Revelation 13:8.

[282] John 3:18.

[283] Ephesians 2:3.

says Luther Lee. "Nothing is to be done, nothing can be done, to make Him any more willing to be gracious than He now is, and always has been." "The problem," he says, is that "we need to be willing to be saved in God's way." This man cannot and will not do by his own free will and strength; therefore, he adds, "the disposition to seek God, is a result of His gracious work already begun in us."[284] Without this work, man may be more than willing to be saved, but never willing to be saved in God's way. Therefore, man's desire to be saved in some other way (one that excludes a subjective transformation of the heart, along with an objective change whereby God declares the sinner righteous), will ever be utilized by some, giving rise to nominal Christianity that allows it to accommodate more customers.

Christ is the Mediator of the New Covenant. All of the blessings of God must be conferred through Him. And all of our approach unto God must be through Him and in His name. The blessings conferred in the New Covenant include union, communion and conformity. As we have already said, those who rejoice solely that their sins are forgiven – past, present and future – care not whether their communion can be disrupted by these future sins, and therefore reject the present ministry of the Mediator. They have embraced another gospel that desires the Mediator only for His benefits, rather than for Himself. Those who minimize conformity to Christ through the agency of His Spirit, reject the Mediator along with the His present application of redemption that was gained by His death. To reject any part of the redemption won by Christ and conferred upon us by God through the power of the Spirit is the despise the price that He paid by His death on the cross and to invent another mediator according to our own desires.

It is only Christ (the God-man) who can settle the claims of both God and man. As perfect, sinless man He could satisfy the divine justice by having the wrath of God poured out upon Himself. As God, He can also reconcile man to God by imparting His own nature, thereby removing the hostility that existed in the heart of man, allowing him to embrace God willingly, and not out of compulsion. He is not only "the Lamb of God,

---

[284] Luther Lee, *The Evangelical Pulpit*, Vol. II (Syracuse, N. Y.: Lee & Masters, 1856), 72.

which taketh away the sin of the world,"[285] He is also Jesus (a Savior) who "shall save His people from their sins."[286] As a lamb He takes the penalty of our sin, as Savior He liberates us from its tyranny.

His ministry of reconciliation is always two-sided. As Mediator, he can remove the enmity that exists in both parties towards each other through the effectual means of His threefold mediatorial offices of Prophet, Priest, and King. As Priest, he acts towards God for man to pacify His wrath and purchase grace for man. As Prophet and King, He acts toward man for God to guide him into God's will and rule him by His Word and Spirit. If we reject any of these three offices of His mediatorial ministry, we reject Him as Mediator and have not yet been reconciled to God, for we are still at enmity with the Mediator Himself and His way of salvation. It is this enmity that must be removed, if we are to be reconciled to God. For Christ's mediatorial offices encompasses the whole of salvation. To deny any of these offices, in either our doctrine or life, is to deny all His work. Therefore, William Guthrie describes such people, who would divide the offices of Christ, as either hypocrites or reprobates,

> As hypocrites and reprobates never close with Christ alone, so they never fully close with Christ as anointed to be King, to rule over a man in all things; a Priest, to procure pardon and to make peace for man upon all occasions; a Prophet, to be wisdom, and a teacher and counselor in all cases to man; so they do not receive Christ, especially in the first and third offices. But where true justifying faith is, a man closeth wholly with Christ in all His offices.[287]

While it is true that it was 2000 years ago on the cross "that God was in Christ reconciling the world unto Himself, not imputing their trespasses unto them,"[288] and that it is a reconciliation received, and therefore already

---

[285] John 1:29.

[286] Matthew 1:21.

[287] William Guthrie, *The Christian's Great Interest* (London: The Banner of Truth Trust, 1982; original 1658), 74.

[288] 2 Corinthians 5:19.

accomplished for them and extended to them from God's side,[289] and that "now hath He reconciled"[290] and not we ourselves, from our side, however, we are not yet reconciled to God unless we have obeyed the command to "be reconciled to God."[291] Otherwise, there would be no present need for the "ministry of reconciliation" to men at all,[292] nor any need of ambassadors[293] to implore man on Christ's behalf to be reconciled to God.[294]

This does not imply that man, by obeying the command to be reconciled to God, moves God to reconcile Himself with man. Rather, our being reconciled to Him is the fruit His being reconciled to us; "we love Him, because He first loved us."[295] But love on our part towards Him, although not the cause, is just as essential for the reality of reconciliation as is His redeeming love towards us. There is nothing meritorious in our reconciling, for the death of Christ on the cross is the sole cause of this single, albeit two-sided, reconciliation. And unless reconciliation be two-sided, it does not exist. In other words, essential to salvation are both

---

[289] Romans 5:11.

[290] Colossians 1:21.

[291] 2 Corinthians 5:20.

[292] 2 Corinthians 5:18.

[293] 2 Corinthians 5:20.

[294] "Although God the Father hath transacted all these things from eternity, and that Jesus Christ hath long since performed all that which might pacify and reconcile His Father, and procure our atonement with His Father, according to the command and request of the Father; yet it was withal mutually then by them, that not a man, no not an elect man, should have benefit by either, until they come in to be reconciled." Thomas Goodwin, *Works of Thomas Goodwin*, Vol. VI (Edinburgh: The Banner of Truth Trust, 1979), 122."Therefore, though our reconciliation to Him is no cause of His reconciliation to us, yet, according to the method which He hath settled as most agreeable to His glorious majesty, to His pure holiness, His hatred of Sin, the justice of His government and the truth of His Word, we cannot say He is actually reconciled to us till we are reconciled to Him. It may be said He pities us before, and is upon gospel-terms reconcilable to us; not that He delights in us or is reconciled." John Howe, *The Works of John Howe, M. A.*, Vol. IV (London: Religious Tract Society, 1872), 393.

[295] 1 John 4:19.

justification and regeneration, and neither of these are earned, but freely bestowed by grace through faith. Christ alone imparts the faith that saves, and the faith that saves always unites the soul with Christ.[296] A. W. Pink writes,

> Mutual alienation, requires mutual reconciliation.…... While a great deal has been written to show that in the transactions between the Father and the Mediator God determined to take full satisfaction unto His justice, and therefore ordained that His Son should be offered a sacrifice, much less has been written to demonstrate that the holiness of God required we must cease our revolt against Him before He can be reconciled to us or receive us into His favor. Yet the one is as true, as important, as necessary, as essential as is the other.[297]

"And you, that were sometime alienated and enemies…yet now hath He reconciled."[298] It is only those who <u>were</u> once alienated and enemies that are <u>now</u> reconciled. Unless we have come to see ourselves in a state of enmity with God, we will never seek a proper reconciliation to Him. Consumer-driven Christianity by-passes that which is the greatest gift God can offer to man in Christ (union and communion with Himself); "Christ also hath once suffered for sins, the just for the unjust, that He might bring us to God."[299] They immediately began to encourage men to seek Him for the lesser things, imagining that there is little or no enmity in man at all. They become seeker-sensitive without realizing that "there

---

[296] "To make perfect reconciliation (which Christ is said in many places to do) it is required, first, that the wrath of God be turned away, His anger removed and all the effects of enmity on His part towards us. Secondly, that we be turned away from our opposition to Him and brought into voluntary obedience. Until both these be effected reconciliation is not perfected." John Owen, from *The Studies in the Scriptures*, 1946 (Carlisle: The Banner of Truth Trust, 1882), 19.

[297] A. W. Pink, *Studies in the Scriptures*, 1946 (Carlisle: The Banner of Truth Trust, 1982; original, 1946), 18.

[298] Colossians 1:21.

[299] 1 Peter 3:18.

is none that seeketh after God."[300] They say, "if man could but see what a benefit it is to serve such a God, they would surely come to Him." Thus, they attempt to lure men to God through the carnal mind that is at enmity against Him.[301] Christ is offered without the necessity of a real reconciliation, because man might be offended if we reveal to him his true nature and need for radical change.

This one-sided reconciliation sells well. It makes all the problem to center on God's side, and implies that man has always been willing and waiting to respond to the opportunity to reconcile with God, which is now made available to him in Christ. All that is needed is for them to learn of God's willingness. If this is all the extent of the gospel that we preach, we render reconciliation impossible. Even Pharaoh, who cared nothing for the God of Israel, could seek Him for the lesser things. He cried out amid his troubles,

> I have sinned against the Lord your God, and against you. Now therefore forgive, I pray thee, my sin only this once, and intreat the Lord your God, that He may take away from me this death only.[302]

He sought God much like a modern consumer, desiring only to use His services, but disregarding His Person, with only a superficial awareness of his total enmity toward God. Good news, for such a one, would consist merely of all that God can do for him, while excluding all that God will do in him. Reconciliation, on the other hand, implies a union with God of heart and wills; of purpose and desire. It implies that one has been drawn to God by the alluring brightness of His glory. True reconciliation reconciles the sinner to the very nature of God, and causes one to embrace and approve of all that God is,[303] and not merely the services that He could render on one's behalf.

Because of Christ's atoning death on the cross, God does not approach

---

[300] Romans 3:11.

[301] Romans 8:7.

[302] Exodus 10:16,17.

[303] "Such as are redeemed are reconciled to God. The enmity is taken away. Their judgment approve, their wills incline ad bonum." Thomas Watson, *A Body of Divinity* (Grand Rapids: Sovereign Grace Publications; reprint), 148.

man as a consuming fire, but rather from the posture of a loving Father, with His arms opened wide, ready to embrace all who come to Him. But only those who come to Him with their arms laid down in unconditional surrender, and not as rebels seeking a truce, or partners in business seeking a deal. Therefore, the distinguishing characteristics of the work of God in the soul is not to reconcile God with our consumer nature, but our consumer nature with the essential characteristics of His Divine nature.

Deliverance from Sin: A 3-Fold Deliverance

It is not primarily from the discomfort, suffering, and troubles of this life, but from the power, penalty and ultimately the presence of sin that He delivers us. It relates not only to our standing, but also to our state. "The whole world lies under the sway of the wicked one."[304] Unless we have been delivered from the desires, pursuits and goals of this world, we are still under its dominion, and cannot comfort ourselves with the hope of that future deliverance from the presence of sin that God has reserved for those whom He has already delivered from the power of darkness and transferred into the kingdom of His Son.[305] Those still in a state of enmity with God will have no standing at all before Him on that day, for they have none in this day.[306]

The sin of this present evil age is idolatry, or the undervaluing of God, which is the greatest evil. The cause of idolatry is the depravity of our hearts. Reconciliation brings God back to the center. Once this change of center has taken place in the heart, our desires, hopes, aims, fears, joys, sorrows and conduct are also changed. We cease to seek salvation merely as liberation from poverty, loneliness or low self-esteem. For true conversion turned our hearts from seeking its greatest happiness in self or the world,

---

[304] 1 John 5:19 NKJV.

[305] Colossians 1:13.

[306] "It is very striking to notice that of the many announcements made concerning the work Christ came to accomplish, nearly every one declares it to be the deliverance from sin, rather than escape from punishment. It is salvation to holiness, rather than salvation to heaven. Of course punishment is escaped, and heaven gained, in the nature of things, when we are saved from sin; since the greater always involves the lesser." Hannah Whitall Smith, *The Open Secret* (New York: Fleming Revell Company, 1885), 91.

as we embrace the source of all true happiness, Christ. As we draw our happiness from this new source, the old source begins to dry up. This is how Christ delivers us from all our idolatries, by taking His rightful place in our heart. He thus restores our happiness by first restoring our holiness. He cannot make us happy with Himself, unless he first makes us holy like Himself. From our side, reconciliation is possible only through regeneration. He removes our enmity by implanting a new heart, thereby restoring our amity.[307]

Those who desire deliverance only from the penalty of sin, desire a partial deliverance, which God never intended. For His act of deliverance cannot contradict the essential perfections of His nature. God's nature is communicated to the believer, not in its essence, but in an inner disposition like unto His own.[308] Therefore, anyone who rests content with deliverance from the penalty of sin, while ignoring that deliverance from the power of sin, cannot possess a disposition like God's, which abominates sin. Wilhelmus a Brakel affirms the inseparableness of salvation from personal holiness when he writes,

> whomever God chooses unto salvation, He also chooses unto holiness.[309]

The Scriptures assert the same, "Now hath he reconciled....", in order "....to present you holy."[310] None can be said to desire reconciliation with a holy God, who refuse holiness in their hearts and lives.

---

[307] "Not only the enmity that is in God is done away, but the Lord also takes away the enmity on the soul's part; that is, you come by virtue of this reconciliation to be so overpowered by the Spirit of God that you have a heart in amity with God..... God puts a reconcilable spirit in you, as He Himself has a reconcilable spirit towards you." Jeremiah Burroughs, *Gospel Reconciliation* (Morgan: Soli Deo Gloria Publications, 1997; original, 1657), 22.

[308] "The most of God's People are contented to be saved from the hell that is without. They are not so anxious to be saved from the hell that is within." *Memoir and Remains of the Rev. Robert Murray M'Cheyne* (Edinburgh: William Oliphant and CO., 1867), 203.

[309] Wilhelmus a Brakel, *The Christians Reasonable Service*, Vol. I (Morgan: Soli Deo Gloria Publications, 1992; original 1700), 240.

[310] Colossians 1:21,22.

Many, and rightly so, consider themselves freed from the penalty of sin and clothed solely in that perfect righteousness of Christ. But for all those for whom this is truly the case, they are also to reckon themselves dead to sins power.[311] The deliverance from the power of sin is not something we are to strive for, it is the work that God has already accomplished for us by imparting a new nature that strives against sin. The believer is to reckon this fact as true, as he strives to live a life free from all acts of sin in word, thought or deed.[312] For while sin no longer rules or reigns, it does remain. While we cannot continue in sin, allowing it to reign in our life as it did before conversion,[313] we may fall into sin, even deplorable ones. Whenever this occurs, God still views us through the lens of Christ's righteousness alone. But because of our new relationship with Him as a Father, He must deal with us as sons and lovingly administer His chastening, which is often grievous, but is for our profit, that we might be partakers of His holiness.[314] Therefore, those who are not partakers of either His discipline or His holiness, cannot be His sons.

Being counted righteous does not imply that we, nor God, ignore our sinful actions; rather, it increases our mutual responsibility. It is totally consistent for the one who is counted righteous to cry out "O wretched man that I am!"[315] But it is only from the framework of the deliverance that God has already accomplished for us in our union with Himself in Christ that holds the key to our walk of holiness, and not what we can achieve through human effort alone. Therefore, those who are truly righteous will also cry out, "I thank God through Jesus Christ our Lord."[316] And these two cries must always accompany reconciliation, for growth in grace is not acceptance of defeat.[317]

It is Christ alone who delivers us, whether that deliverance be from either the guilt or the power of sin. Thomas Manton affirms that the work of Christ accomplishes both when he writes,

---

[311] Romans 6:11

[312] Hebrews 12:4

[313] Romans 6:1-7

[314] Hebrews 12:7-11

[315] Romans 7:24

[316] Romans 7:25

[317] Romans 8

Christ' blood was not only a price, but a laver wherein
to wash us and make us clean....and Christ came not
only to abolish the guilt of sin against our interest, our
peace, our comfort, but also to destroy the power of sin,
which is against God's glory.[318]

Although it is solely the power of grace that delivers, the delivered
life is anything but an effortless life.[319] The narrow gate of justification
always leads to the narrow way of sanctification. While we are not saved by
works, we are saved for works.[320] By imputing His own righteousness, God
intends to exclude all boasting. By imparting His own nature, He intends
to include a life characterized by that righteousness. But all efforts towards
a life of righteousness are God-dependent, performed solely as we abide
in Christ, without whom we can do nothing.[321] The only proper attitude
toward all of the efforts on our part will forevermore be:

Unto him that loved us, and washed us from our sins
in His own blood....be glory and dominion forever and
ever. Amen.[322]

Nothing in my hand I bring
simply to Thy cross I cling.

Christ must remain the central focus of the delivered, even above the
deliverance that they received. Our deliverance is the primary purpose
of redemption only insofar as it promotes God's glory. The glory of the
Gospel is not that it provides for man's happiness, but that it does so in
such a way that promotes God's glory. Those who invent a Christianity
that minimizes the need for a life of holiness, reject the end of the gospel
and do not contribute toward the happiness of man. "For we are His

---

[318] Thomas Manton, Commentary on Jude (Grand Rapids: Kregel
Publications, 1988; original, 1658), 40.
[319] 1 Corinthians 9:24-27
[320] Ephesians 2:8-10
[321] John 15:5.
[322] Revelations 1:5,6.

workmanship"[323] only if we bear the image of His Son. Thus, He secures our highest happiness by drawing us away from our consumer existence, and unto the glory of God. What is at stake in having only a consumer view of redemption is nothing short of an attack on the preeminence of Christ. Those who reject a two-fold reconciliation, or a three-fold deliverance, have no intention of cherishing the preeminence of Christ above the counterfeit offers of a consumer driven Christianity. Therefore, opting rather to exchange a Christianity of loving God with all their heart, soul, mind, and strength, they prefer one that encourages the supreme love of self.

---

[323] Ephesians 2:10.

CHAPTER 8

Faith's Glorious Vision –Its Agent

> At that time Jesus answered and said, I thank thee O Father, Lord of heaven and earth, because Thou hast hid these things from the wise and prudent, and hast revealed them unto babes. Even so, Father: for so it seemed good in Thy sight. All things are delivered unto unto Me of My Father: and no man knoweth the Son, but the Father; neither knoweth any man the Father, save the Son, and he to whosoever the Son will reveal Him.
>
> Matthew 11:25 – 27

Total depravity means that man is totally unable to deliver himself. Self-deliverance (or in modern terminology self-help) is a contradiction in terms. Self cannot deliver us, because it is from self that we need deliverance. The only help that self seeks is improvement. But salvation is not improvement, it is deliverance. This deliverance can only begin when we acknowledge the Spirit as its sole Agent, and humbly recognize our utter helplessness and sinfulness. Those who fail to recognize this simple fact, will continue to look to themselves or other means for deliverance.

The Spirit's work of illumination, wrought prior to regeneration, is to convict the world of sin, of righteousness and of judgment,[324] Before reconciliation is possible, man must be irreconcilable to himself. If we

---

[324] John 16:8 – 11.

trust in our own sufficiency, we remain spiritually blind to His true glory. His command is:

> Look to Me, and be ye saved, all the ends of the earth:
> for I am God, and there is none else.[325]

One can only be saved as he looks to God, and away from self and all else for his salvation. "The only true knowledge of God is that which is given to faith," says John Thomas, "it is the vision of the eternal beauty of infinite truth and love."[326] Saving faith is more than a speculative look or curious gaze. It involves the earnestness that accompanies a deep sense of one's utter inability and absolute need for Christ. The preaching of the gospel, then, can only be effective in the salvation of sinners as it provides the man-humbling and God-exalting knowledge that such a faith presupposes. And, as it depends upon the work of the Spirit to render such knowledge effectual by opening the eyes of the understanding to perceive this knowledge, it must always go forth with that dependence upon the Spirit that prayer for deliverance presupposes. False prayer may cry out to God for help, but since these prayers are not self-emptying, they do not look to God alone.

Divine revelation and natural revelation have this in common, they both "declare the glory of God."[327] Looking to God, in any saving way, always involves a true spiritual perception of His glory. While the unregenerate may perceive God's existence and attributes as revealed in creation,[328] being blind to their true glory, these truths are suppressed. Speaking of the Spirit of truth, the apostle John says,

> whom the world cannot receive, because it seeth Him
> not, neither knoweth Him.[329]

If they could but see the same beauty in God as they see in the world

---

[325] Isaiah 45:22.

[326] John Thomas, *The Dynamic of the Cross*, (London: H. R. Allenson), 108.

[327] Psalm 19:1.

[328] Romans 1:18 – 22.

[329] John 14:17.

or self, they would follow as hard after Him as they follow the world or self. But the glory of the Lord far surpasses that of the world as the sun outshines the stars. As the blind man is blind to the light of the sun, so the unregenerate are blind to the light of God's glory. Blinded by their own enmity, they cannot see the alluring brightness of His glory, but only that which repels. Again, the apostle John says,

> For every one that doeth evil hateth the light, neither cometh to the light, lest his deeds should be reproved.[330]

No man will acknowledge that as true, which he hates for being contrary to himself, for all men are blinded by a natural bias towards themselves. His enmity against the light will only acknowledge a god he has invented; a false god, acceptable to his depraved nature; one who does not call him to utterly deny himself and forsake his ways, but rather calls him to embrace himself and affirms his ways. While gross sins may be weakened, the stronghold of self-idolatry remains strong.

We assume that sinful man will not respond unless we preach a gospel that exalts the benefits and lowers the responsibilities. And we assume right. For none will respond without a supernatural work of grace. Jesus boldly proclaimed,

> No man can come to Me, except the Father which hath sent Me draw him.[331]

Therefore, from our thirst and impatience to increase our numbers, we invent ways to lure men without this supernatural work. And once these affirmed men have entered the church without any supernatural change of nature, we must continue to minimize the requirements and exalt the benefits in order to keep them there. If this were not enough, we use every means at our disposal to keep them interested; such as entertainment, dramas, music, self-help classes, enticing words of human wisdom, among others. Whenever the church depends on such techniques to enlarge its membership, it reveals its own opposition to its original design. What

---

[330] John 3:20.
[331] John 6:44.

the consumer-driven church is really promoting is neither Christ nor the gospel, but the church as they have reinvented it for market. Consumerism may lead some to take up religion, but it will never lead them to take up the cross. The unbeliever is drawn to the church, not Christ. While merely joining themselves to the body, they are guilty of "not holding the Head."[332]

Whenever this vendor/consumer relationship exists, we transform Christianity and the church into commodities that appeal to man's self-love. Like an illicit relationship where there is not that self-denial that the marriage vows entail, one must, like a commodity, constantly sell oneself, or the other party may be tempted to end the relationship and shop for more gratifying goods elsewhere. Wherever the church utilizes this vendor-consumer model in reaching the lost, the church becomes the agent and its power of persuasion becomes the instrument of man's salvation, thus eliminating the need for any special assistance of the Spirit in effectual calling. We begin to employ evangelistic tools that attempt to either improve the clear preaching of the Gospel or enhance the powerful agency of the Holy Spirit in saving souls. While none can so limit God as to say that He cannot work despite such methods, all do limit God who depend upon some new method or the power of persuasion above the ability of God to draw sinners unto Himself. And all do limit His regenerating power, who are satisfied with forging a mere illicit, superficial and temporary relationship where commitment is lacking, and self-gratification is the goal.

God does not solicit our selfishness and consumer interest when drawing us unto Himself, and then afterwards reveal the sinfulness of these inordinate dispositions that He at first used to bring us unto Himself. This misconstrues the nature of the new birth. Appealing to the flesh does not make it possible for God to draw us unto Himself. In the scheme of salvation, "the flesh profiteth nothing."[333] What is impossible for man is not made possible by the flesh. For those who are the sons of God "were born, not of blood, nor of the will of the flesh, nor of the will of man, but of God."[334]

---

[332] Colossians 2:19.
[333] John 6:63.
[334] John 1:12 – 13.

God effectually draws men to Christ only by His Word and Spirit. It is not until the eyes of our understanding are opened by the Spirit, through the word, at regeneration, that the glory of the Lord is perceived by the eye of faith. There must first be a new nature implanted in the soul like God's, before we can see any beauty in the nature of God that would draw us to Him. Until such a time, one may be driven out of fear or self-love, but not drawn by "faith, which worketh by love,"[335] rather than coercion. G. S. Faber explains why coercion never works,

> No human argument can persuade a man to love what he hates, and to delight in what he detests. Submission they may perhaps teach him; but it will be the sullen submission of a slave, not the cheerful acquiescence of a son.[336]

Coercion is nothing more than an attempt to produce an outward response by forces that are outside of ourselves. These external forces are applied to get us to do what we would not normally desire to do by nature. Regeneration, on the other hand, produces the outer by implanting an inner nature that now desires the outer for its own sake, and not merely as the means to anything that we esteem greater.

Since our nature is totally depraved it must be totally changed, or man will not come. We must be born again before we can even see,[337] much less enter the kingdom of God.[338] There must first be a new nature implanted in the heart, before there can be a new and opposite knowledge; new, not in the notional sense of it, but as it now engages the heart as well as the head. According to William Ames, it is possible to have a correct head-knowledge that does not touch the heart,[339]

> The offer of Christ is outward and inward. The outward in the preaching of the gospel or the promises of Christ....

---

[335] Galatians 5:6.

[336] G. S. Faber, *A Practical Treatise on the Ordinary Operations of the Holy Spirit* (New York: Eastburn, Kirk and Co, 1814), xii.

[337] John 3:3.

[338] John 3:5.

[339] Revelations 2:2 – 4.

> The inward offer is a kind of spiritual enlightenment,
> whereby the promises are presented to the hearts of men,
> as it were, by an inner word (John 6:45, Eph 1:17,18).[340]

Archibald Alexander also distinguishes between these two very different types of knowledge,

> Speculative or mere natural knowledge of scriptural
> truths - not penetrating into the true excellence of the
> truths believed, but resting on the external evidences
> and systematic relations of the truth, exercise little
> influence on the heart and affections, whereas spiritual
> or saving knowledge, by which the beauty and glory
> of divine things are apprehended, has the immediate
> effect of exciting the affections and emotions in a way
> corresponding with the nature of the objects perceived.
> Under the influence of new and holy feelings, the
> purpose of the heart to honor, worship, and obey God
> is formed, and this purpose becomes habitual; and the
> clearer the soul's views of divine things, the firmer and
> stronger this purpose becomes.[341]

A notional knowledge of God is insufficient to change the flow of our affections. This kind of knowledge alone is deceptive to those who possess it, simply because they possess it. "Certainly, my knowledge and interest in spiritual things is proof of my spiritually, for I am more knowledgeable and zealous in these matters than most." But it is not the degree of your knowledge that matters. It is the nature of it. You may have a high degree of notional knowledge concerning the attributes of God, with a low appreciation of those attributes. Even the knowledge of God revealed in the Gospel, while embraced in the head, may be suppressed in the heart. The consequence of a true knowledge of God is always costly. It is possible

---

[340] William Ames, *The Marrow of Theology* (Grand Rapids: Baker Books, 1997; original, 1623), 158.

[341] Archibald Alexander, *Practical Sermons to be Read in Families and Social Meetings* (Philadelphia: Presbyterian Board of Publications, 1850), 10 – 11.

to have a correct notional understanding of God without a desire to pay the price that this knowledge demands. This kind of knowledge is so far from being a saving knowledge that even the demons possess it.[342] Although a saving knowledge includes objective knowledge, it is not to be confused with it. A. W. Pink expressed it this way:

> A saving knowledge is not a knowledge of divine things,
> but a divinely imparted knowledge.[343]

Richard Sibbes attributes this divine work to the Spirit when he writes,

> It is not enough to know by the Word that there is strength and righteousness in Christ, but the Spirit must open the eyes of the soul, else we shall only have a natural knowledge of supernatural things. It is necessary to have a supernatural sight to see supernatural things.[344]

John Bunyan, in "The Pilgrim's Progress", describes the second encounter of Christian and Hopeful with a fellow called Ignorance. After discovering how willfully ignorant he was as to the objective way of salvation, they proceeded to question him about that subjective saving knowledge that is both internal and spiritual in nature:

---

[342] James 2:19.

[343] A W Pink, *The Holy Spirit* (Grand Rapids: Baker Book House, 1972), 101

[344] Richard Sibbes, *Divine Meditation and Holy Contemplations* (London: J. Buckland, 1775), 83.

Hopeful. Ask him if ever he had Christ revealed to him from heaven.[345]

Ignorance. What! You are a man for revelations! I do believe that what both you and all the rest of you say about that matter is but the fruit of distracted brains.

Hopeful. Why, man! Christ is so hid in God from the natural apprehensions of the flesh, that He cannot by any man be savingly known, unless God the Father reveals Him to them.

Ignorance. That is your faith, but not mine: yet mine, I doubt not, is as good as yours, though I have not in my head so many whimsies as you.

Christian. Give me leave to put in a word: You ought not to speak so slightly of this matter: for this I boldly affirm, (even as my good companion hath done,) that no man can know Jesus Christ but by the revelation of the Father; yea, and faith too, by which the soul layeth hold upon Christ, (if it be right,) must be wrought by the exceeding greatness of His mighty power, (Matt. xi.27; 1 Cor xiii. 3; Eph. i. 18,19;) the working of which faith, I perceive, poor Ignorance, thou art ignorant of.[346]

---

[345] The footnote from the 1873 Bradley, Garretson and Co. edition of *The Pilgrim's Progress* explains in greater detail what this revelation of Christ includes: "It pleased God to reveal His Son in me, (Gal. 1:16) that is, he had such an internal, spiritual, experimental sight and knowledge of Christ, and salvation by Him, that his heart embraces Him, his soul cleaves to Him, his spirit rejoices in Him; his whole man was swallowed up with the love of Him, so that he cried out in the joy of his soul, This is my Beloved and my Friend, my Savior, my God, and my Salvation. He is the Chief of ten thousand, and altogether lovely. We know nothing of Christ savingly, comfortably, and experimentally, till He is pleased thus to reveal Himself to us. Matt. xi. 27."

[346] John Bunyan, *The Complete Works of John Bunyan* (Philadelphia: Bradley, Garretson and Co., 1873), 163.

Jonathan Edwards also confirms that no degree of speculative knowledge would avail without this supernatural revelation of Christ to the heart,

> No degree of speculative knowledge of religion is any certain sign of true piety. Whatever clear notions a man may have of the attributes of God, the doctrine of the Trinity, the nature of the two covenants, the economy of the persons of the Trinity, and the part which each person has in the affairs of man's redemption; if he can discourse never so excellently of the offices of Christ, the way of salvation by Him, the admirable methods of divine wisdom, and the harmony of the various attributes of God in that way; if he can talk never so clearly and exactly of the method of the justification of a sinner, of the nature of conversion, and the operations of the Spirit of God in applying the redemption of Christ, giving good distinction, happily solving difficulties, and answering objections, in a manner tending greatly to enlighten the ignorant, to the edification of the church of God, the conviction of gainsayers, and the great increase of light in the world; if he has more knowledge of this sort than hundreds of true saints of an ordinary education, and most divines, yet all is no certain evidence of any degree of saving grace in the heart.[347]

Until eternal life is imparted into the soul by the Holy Spirit, the true knowledge of God cannot even commence.[348] The natural man may know facts about God, but those who possess eternal life know God. "And this is life eternal, that they might know Thee the only true God, and Jesus Christ whom Thou hast sent."[349] Eternal life, then, consists in the knowledge of God. The knowledge that is imparted in regeneration is

---

[347] Jonathan Edwards, *The True Believer* (Morgan: Soli Deo Gloria Publications, 2001), 28.
[348] 1 Corinthians 2:11 – 14.
[349] John 17:3.

a spiritual knowledge.[350] The results of such a knowledge is not merely an intellectual prayer to calm our fears, but a desperate plea that engages the whole of our being, and leaves the soul forever changed. It sets man free not merely because he knows it to be true, but because he values it above those things that bind him.

The true knowledge of God, imparted by the Spirit, produces true love for Him. This is the knowledge of God that is implied in reconciliation, because it restores that communion with God that had been destroyed by sin. Thus, it consists not only of right facts, but also endearing affections. "True knowledge and pious affections," writes Archibald Alexander, "are inseparably conjoined; the one cannot exist without the other."[351] It is not enough to know about the preeminence of Christ, we must "approve things that are excellent,"[352] if we are to cherish in our hearts the excellent knowledge of Christ above all lesser things.

> "There is implied in the idea of the beautiful something engaging, alluring, something which attracts the hearts towards itself and makes us love to linger on it…..We cannot look upon Him aright without loving Him and feeling ourselves drawn towards Hi."[353]

---

[350] Colossians 3:10.

[351] Archibald Alexander, *Practical Sermons to be Read in Families and Social Meetings* (Philadelphia: Presbyterian Board of Publications, 1850), 22.

[352] Philippians 1:10.

[353] The Reformed Presbyterian Magazine (Edinburgh: Johnstone and Hunter; 1855), 275.

CHAPTER 9

Faith's Glorious Vision
– Its Instrument

Of His own will begat He us with the word of truth,
that we should be a kind of firstfruits of His creatures....
Wherefore lay apart all filthiness and superfluity of
naughtiness, and receive with meekness the engrafted
Word, which is able to save your souls.

James 1:18,21

Being born again, not of corruptible seed, but of
incorruptible, by the Word of God, which liveth and
abideth for ever.

1 Peter 2:23

We love Him whom we have not seen, because the Bible reveals the
loveliness of His Person, which in turn draws the affections toward
His beauty. Regeneration does not provide the knowledge that our faith
embraces. This is provided only through the instrumentality of the Word,
whether read or heard. But it does align our affections and will with the
Word. A heart aflame with love is impossible without an informed head.
An informed head alone, however clear and precise, cannot reach the
heart without the eye of faith. "Now faith is the substance of things hoped

for, the evidence of things not seen."[354] It is with the eye of faith that we behold the glory of God shining forth through the Word. God can be known by the eye of faith only in the light of His own revelation. Since none are acquainted with God but He Himself, we must depend on His own revelation of Himself in order to know Him.

Although mere speculative knowledge, in and of itself, is no distinguishing characteristic of regeneration, it is a necessary characteristic of all those who are truly regenerate. The Word of God alone is the lens through which the eye of faith beholds the excellencies of God and the way of salvation by Him. Therefore, those who deny objective truth are incapable of perceiving His glory expressed through the Word. For if there is no absolute truth, as many affirm, then God cannot be known.

Although speculative knowledge is vital to the true knowledge God, Edward Griffin asserts that something must be included along with it,

> The knowledge which I would recommend, though it includes the speculation of the understanding, is not confined to it. It consists in a clear discernment of God's spiritual glory and a holy intimacy with Him; which can be obtained neither by a speculative knowledge without right affections, nor yet by warm affections without deep and extensive knowledge.[355]

Therefore, a correct objective knowledge, to some degree, is indispensable for a correct love for God, since embracing a false notion of Him produces a false love for Him, consisting in much activity, but possessing little value. "Ye do err, not knowing the scriptures", was Christ's evaluation of the Sadducees.[356] Thomas Manton gives the same assessment of the danger that erroneous objective knowledge poses on the affections,

> He can never shoot right that takes his aim contrary. The understanding directs all the inferior powers of the

---

[354] Hebrews 11:1.

[355] Edward Griffin, *Sermons by the Late Edward Griffin D.D.*, Vol. I (New York: John S Taylor, 1839), 274.

[356] Matthew 22:29.

soul; if that is infected with error, the affections must necessarily move out of order.[357]

It is crucial, then, that we discover whether our knowledge of God is a saving one or not. This task is not as easy as some suppose, but it is not as difficult as others suppose.[358] Jesus describes many who will come to Him in the last day having done much religious activity, of whom He will declare, "I never knew you."[359] There were ten virgins waiting, but to five of them He said, "I know you not."[360] There were two foundations laid; same activity, different results.[361] There are the wheat and the tares; same appearance, but different natures.[362] When Christ returns, there will be such a mixture of the righteous and the wicked that it will be necessary to "sever the wicked from among the just."[363] The test of the foundation of our faith is "whoever hears these sayings of Mine and does them."[364] There are many who love to hear the Word of God, but seek no reformation of heart. Like Joash, they are influenced by others to an outward reform, but once these people are removed, their hypocrisy is revealed.[365] All our orthodoxy is in vain if it makes no alteration on the heart. "The special intent of the ministry," says Richard Sibbes, "is to work upon the heart and affections."[366]

Hypocrisy is always the tendency of consumerism when mixed with religion. Ezekiel prophesied,

---

[357] Thomas Manton, *One Hundred and Ninety Sermons on the Hundred and Ninteeth Psalm* (London: William Brown, 1845), 196.

[358] "Immense is the difference between an intellectual knowledge and a real experience of the truth, which maketh wise unto salvation." J.J. Van Oosterzee, *Christian Dogmatics* (London: Hodder and Stoughton, 1874), 675.

[359] Matthew 7:21 – 23.

[360] Matthew 25:1 – 12.

[361] Matthew 7:24 – 29.

[362] Matthew 13:24 – 30.

[363] Matthew 13:49.

[364] Matthew 7:24.

[365] 2 Chronicles 24:2 – 18.

[366] Sibbes, *Divine Meditations*, 147.

> They speak to one another, everyone saying to his
> brother, 'Please come and hear what the Word is that
> comes from the Lord.' So they come to you as people
> do, they sit before you as My people, and they hear your
> words, but they do not do them; for with their mouth
> they show much love, but their hearts pursue their own
> gain. Indeed you are to them as a very lovely song of
> one who has a pleasant voice and can play well on an
> instrument; for they hear your words, but they do not
> do them.[367]

Our hypocrisy deceives more than others. Jonathan Edwards deduces from the Scriptures that it deceives even ourselves;

> Wicked men, in Scripture, are represented as longing
> for the privileges of the righteous when the door is shut,
> and they are shut out from among them. They come to
> the door and cry 'Lord, Lord, open to us'. Therefore,
> we are not to look on all desires that are very earnest
> and vehement as certain evidences of a pious heart...
> They think they hunger and thirst after righteousness,
> have earnest desires after God and Christ, and long for
> heaven, when indeed, all is merely self-love. And so it is
> a longing which arises from no higher principles then
> the earnest desires of devils.[368]

There are many who claim to love God who are indifferent to the study of Him. And this can never be. For to love God with all our minds is to employ all our intellectual capacities in the discovery of Him. Without this we will not be able to thoroughly engage all our affections in the love of Him, nor correctly pour out our strength in the service of Him. Orthodoxy and piety are inseparable. Burning hearts are not nourished by empty heads.

---

[367] Ezekiel 33:30-32 NKJ.

[368] Jonathan Edwards, *The True Believer* (Morgan: Soli Deo Gloria Publications, 2001), 41.

Then again, there are many who are "ever learning, and never able to come to the knowledge of the truth."[369] Many of these are dedicated to theology as a mere academic pursuit, and not for its sanctifying and saving effects. A subject so vast as the study of God cannot produce pride, for He is a deep ocean of which we only possess a drop. Pride is the result of the study of a counterfeit that we have broken down to our finite understanding. The typical theologian that flaunts his vast knowledge and theological innovations misses the purpose and point of Scripture and comes short of that knowledge that is both saving and conducive to loving God with all his heart and his neighbor as himself. These are no different from any other spiritual consumer who uses God for his own purposes. We should not be impressed by those who possess that which even devils possess – vast amounts of biblical knowledge. To be impressed by such knowledge reveals a secret atheism, for the more we live in the presence of God, the less impressed we will be by those things that can be achieved merely through the power of self-love.

The theologian who can debate persuasively and accurately on the extent and intent of the atonement gives no clear evidence of regeneration. Although everything he affirms may be true and beneficial to the church, it may only be a purely academic pursuit. The devil, along with the unregenerate, can understand many things relating to God, but there is something about God that neither the devil nor the wicked can perceive, and that is the true glory and loveliness of God and all His ways. This is only perceived with the heart, and not merely understood with the head. "The natural man receiveth not the things of the Spirit."[370] To perceive this man needs a new heart.[371]

---

[369] 1 Timothy 3:7.

[370] 1 Corinthians 2:14.

[371] Octavius Winslow warns, in his book *"Personal Declension and Revival of Religion,*" that even the regenerate can decline in the passion of the heart without necessarily losing the clarity of the head. "The decay of grace may be advancing without any marked decline in the spiritual perception of judgment, as to the beauty and fitness of spiritual truth. The judgment shall lose none of its light; but the heart much of its fervor; the truth of revelation shall lose none of its light and occupy the same prominent position as to their value and beauty, and yet the influence of these truths may be scarcely felt."

Paul characterizes the lost as those "which know not God,"[372] and the regenerate as those who know Him.[373] And because we know Him, we must love Him, since He is the loveliest Object of knowledge. The spiritual vision imparted in regeneration is not perfect, for the beatific vision is reserved for another world. We only "see through a glass darkly."[374] But we still see something! Although we can never fully perceive the glory of the Lord in its essence, we are still able to perceive that that knowledge is incomprehensible, thus outshining all the glories of the world, turning our hearts God-wards, away from the world. Like the sun, which no man can fully look upon, though all men perceive its glory, God's incomprehensibility only enhances His glory. For if God could be fully understood by finite man, He would cease to be infinitely glorious and not worth knowing at all. For such a god, far from transcending our understanding, would merely be the creation of it.

That which can be known of God, however, are His attributes and works as they are reflected in creation and shine forth through the pages of Scripture. These things not only can be known, they must be known, if we are to perceive His true glory. Without the discovery of these attributes, there can be no true saving knowledge of God. Nor could the saving work of Christ on the cross, which is the display of all these attributes, be readily understood. Archibald Alexander insisted,

> the work of the Spirit, in the regeneration of the heart, is adapted to the rational nature of man. The thing to be accomplished, is not the creation of some new faculty; it is a moral renovation; and all moral changes must be effected by understanding and choices. To put the soul, therefore, in that state in which it will rightly understand the truth, and cordially choose the highest good, is the end of regeneration. Truth, therefore, must

---

[372] 1 Thessalonians 4:5.

[373] Galatians 4:8,9.

[374] 1 Corinthians 3:9.

be the means by which actual conversion to God takes place.[375]

When we direct our gospel towards the consumer, like a salesman declaring that which is designed only to produce a positive response, we conceal the instrumentality of the Word, and reveal our distrust of the agency of the Spirit in illumination, thus producing an emotional response to a god more desirable to the depraved nature. The degree of accuracy in our presentation of the gospel to the understanding of man only increases its effectiveness as the instrument of the Spirit in the conversion of souls. And our degree of inaccuracy accounts for much of the disparity and lack of reality that arise among conversions throughout the church. If the truth they receive from the gospel we preach is directed towards their consumer interest, how will those who embrace this message be converted from their consumer attitude of "Me first"?

This disparity, because of man's depraved heart, exist even when the Word is preached with unmistakable clarity, for there are many grounds where the Word is sown that produce no fruit at all.[376] Only "he that heareth the Word, and understandeth it....beareth fruit". How little fruit, then, might be expected from seed that has been tainted by a consumer-driven gospel? Although the Spirit is sovereign in the conversion of man, He works through the instrumentality of the Word. And our conversion usually takes the shape of the words in which our faith confides. All true conversions are alike in essence, but all are very different in degree. Even the Word that falls on good ground brings forth fruit in varying degrees, "some an hundred-fold, some sixty, some thirty."[377]

Because of the depravity of man's heart, the Spirit must not only prepare the messenger who proclaims the Word, He must also prepare the heart to receive it. The greatest advantage in obtaining a saving knowledge of God is not intellectual superiority, but a disposition to do His will.[378] And this disposition is only giver by the Spirit in regeneration. There is no

---

[375] Archibald Alexander, from *Advice to a Young Christian* (New York: The American Tract Society, 1843), 8.
[376] Matthew 13:18 – 23.
[377] Matthew 13:23.
[378] John 7:17, Matthew 11:25 – 27.

greater sign of self-deception, than a lack of this disposition: "not hearers only deceiving your own selves."[379] Archibald Alexander further explains,

> True religion not only enlightens the understanding, but rectifies the affections of the heart. All genuine feelings of piety are the effects of divine truth. The variety and intensity of these feelings depend on the different kinds of truth, and the various aspects in which the same truth is viewed; and also, on the distinctiveness and clearness with which it is presented to the mind. In a state of moral perfection, truth would uniformly produce all those emotions and affections which correspond with its nature, without the aid of any superadded influence. That these effects are not experienced by all who have the opportunity of knowing the truth, is a strong evidence of human depravity. In a state of moral depravity, the mind is incapable alike of perceiving and feeling the beauty and excellence of divine truth. The dead neither see nor feel, and a man is by nature 'dead in trespasses and sins.' Hence, the necessity of the agency of the Holy Spirit to illuminate and regenerate the mind.[380]

The effectiveness of the word to enlighten depends on how we listen.[381] Basil said: "Men, when they expound Scriptures, always bring something of themselves."[382] If self-love reigns supreme, then we will only hear the message of self-love. We will hear Scripture only as it promotes self. Since we only hear the message of the one whose nature we possess,[383] a corrupt heart cannot receive a holy message.[384] It only comes to the word to satisfy its curiosity, love of learning, or delight in selfishly misconceived benefits, and so only extracts from Scripture what it seeks, himself.

---

[379] James 1:21.
[380] Archibald Alexander, from *Advice to a Young Christian*, 7.
[381] Luke 8:18.
[382] Basil, from The Sermons of the Right Rev. Jeremy Taylor (New York: Robert Carter and Brothers, 1859), 461.
[383] John 8:42 – 47.
[384] 1 John 4:5,6.

All may come to the same Word, but one comes with an eye to self, while the another comes with an eye to God. Hence, they both come to a different word, which produces different effects. Hence, they both perceive a different God in the Word. One sees the beauty of God and His ways, while the other sees how self can be promoted. Selfish hearing will never produce self-denying obedience. One "receives the Word of God......not as the word of men, but as it is in truth, the Word of God, which also effectively works in you who believe."[385] The consumer receives it as a word to a god (himself), for he possesses no true faith in God, and reserves the right to pick and choose, as in some market, whichever part of the Word he prefers. Thus, the deceived consumer only beholds his own selfish desires in the Word, whereas the believer beholds the will of God to which he seeks to conform. Willen Teellinck distinguishes between these two types of hearers,

> Carnal people subject God's Word to their own minds and manipulate it as they see fit, according to their understanding, instead of subordinating and ordering their thoughts and minds so that they are brought into captivity to God's word.[386]

Thus, Consumer-driven Christianity succeeds, because there are many who have no desire to submit to the authority of Scripture and are willing to be enticed by proof-texts that can be taken out of context and manipulated to accord with their desires.

Since the Spirit opposes the flesh,[387] as He promotes God's glory,[388] it is to be assumed that the Word He inspired, the ministry that He empowers and the work that He performs upon the soul will have the same tendency. The flesh brings about a bias towards ourselves. We, then, are bias toward the Word. Even that in the Word which is readily understood is biased towards self, so that the more flesh pleasing side of any truth is

---

[385] 1 Thessalonians 2:13.

[386] Willen Teelinck, *The Path of true Godliness* (Grand Rapids: Baker Academic, 2003; original, 1636), 61.

[387] Galatians 5:17.

[388] John 16:14.

exalted above the part that is more self-denying. If our quest to promote God's glory does not lead us to oppose the flesh, then it cannot be the work of His Spirit. That message which is preached to entice man's selfish nature cannot proceed from the Spirit. We are not drawn by the Spirit, unless we are drawn to Christ by the excellencies of His person and work, and not for our own convenience. If we choose from God's Word at our own convenience, then we believe none of it on the right basis. It is not because God has spoken it that we accept it, but for our own convenience. So, consumer-driven Christianity, whose primary concern is not for the glory of God, cannot proceed from His Spirit.

The consumer-driven church, in order to keep the churches full and the people happy, must be very selective as to which portions of God's Word that are stressed. Like salesmen, those parts of God's Word and nature that are offensive to the customer are watered-down or avoided altogether. But "all Scripture is given by inspiration of God", and it is all Scripture that "is profitable."[389] To reject any of it is to reject all of it. But it is what we believe the Scriptures are profitable for that determines how we hear or proclaim them. Is it profitable for the promotion of our desires, ease and outward success? Or is it "profitable for doctrine, for reproof, for correction, for instruction in righteousness: that the man of God may be perfect, thoroughly furnished unto all good works?"[390] The primary desires of one's heart determines not only what one seeks from the Scriptures, but also what one draws from the Scriptures.

True faith, like true obedience, is impartial. It is the flesh that picks and chooses what to obey, and therefore only serves itself, because it always chooses itself. True faith esteems the whole Word of God. The flesh would have God be true to His promises, yet false to His warnings. But true faith will not take His promises more seriously than His commands and warnings. You do not have faith to believe His promises, if you do not have faith to obey His commands and heed His warnings. How much you believe the Bible in every area, reveals how much you believe the Bible in any area. To reject some of it, is to reject all of it. The flesh takes strength from unbelief, which always reasons its way out of any obedience that is not self-serving. While it may embrace certain truths that are orthodox,

---

[389] 2 Timothy 3:16
[390] 2 Timothy 3:17,18

even these truths, like those who have a form of godliness, are embraced for the service they render in giving the form of orthodoxy that is necessary for service in the church.

If faith has a glorious vision of God, then pseudo faith will have an inglorious one that only centers on self. How can we know if we have a genuine faith? If we have the same faith as Abraham, it will have the same results. "By faith Abraham obeyed."[391] It was Abraham's faith that was tested, but the test was his obedience. How seriously would he take the Word of God? The answer was shown by his obedience. Our faith is as big, or small, as our obedience. True faith need no greater reason to obey other than the fact that God has commanded it. The flesh always seeks some selfish reason to obey. And consumer-driven Christianity incessantly puts forth these reasons, over and above the beauty and glory of Christ, to attract its customers.

The counsel of William Gurnall cuts right to the heart of the two erroneous propositions of consumer-driven Christianity, which once recognized destroys its false foundation. First, by showing that real Christianity is not so pleasing to the flesh, and secondly, by showing that it is not so popular with the masses,

> If profession would serve the turn, and flocking after sermons with some seeming joy at the word were enough to save, heaven would soon be full: but as you love your souls, do not try yourselves by this coarse sieve; that is, seek by an easy profession, and cheap religion, such as is hearing the Word, performance of duties and the like; of the kind there are many that will come and walk about heaven's door, willing enough to enter, if they may do it without ruffling their pride in a crowd, or hazarding their present carnal interest by any contest and scuffle. Take Christians under the notion of "seekers," and, by Christ's own works, there are many; but consider them under the notion of "strivers," such as stand ready shod with a holy resolution, to strive even to blood, if such trails meet them in the way to heaven, rather than not

---

[391] Hebrews 11:8

enter, and then the number of Christian soldiers will shrink, like Gideon's goodly host, to a little troop.[392]

Unless our search for God be disinterested, we will never behold His glory shining forth through the pages of Scripture, but merely the confirmation of our own interests, reflecting from our own hearts out of the pages of Scripture.[393] Therefore, we must "prepare our heart to seek Him,"[394] and "set ourselves to seek the Lord,"[395] knowing that we shall seek Him so as to find Him only after we have laid aside our consumer interest to search for Him with all our heart.[396] "In Scripture," says James Macknight, "seeking denotes the constant employing of one's thoughts and endeavours for obtaining the object of one's desires."[397] God is the Object of our desires, then, only if we constantly employ our thoughts and endeavors in the pursuit of Him, rather than the gratification of self.

---

[392] William Gurnall, *Gleanings from William Gurnall* (Morgan: Soli Deo Gloria Publications, 1996; original, 1941), 21.

[393] Matthew 13:14 – 17.

[394] 2 Chronicles 19:3.

[395] 1 Chronicles 20:3.

[396] Jeremiah 29:13.

[397] James MacKnight, *Apostolical Epistles* (Philadelphia: Thomas Wardle, 1841), 391.

CHAPTER 10

The Saving Knowledge of God – Its Subject

But if our gospel is hid, it is hid to them that are lost, in whom the god of this world hath blinded the minds of them which believe not, lest the light of the glorious gospel of Christ, who is the image of God, should shine unto them.....For God, who commanded the light to shine out of darkness, hath shined in our hearts, to give the light of the knowledge of the glory of God in the face of Jesus Christ.

2 Corinthians 4:3,4,6

Its Subject: The Heart, "hath shined in our hearts."

The distinguishing mark of true saving knowledge is its influence upon the heart. "I will give them a heart to know Me, that I am the Lord: and they shall be My people, and I will be their God: for they shall return unto Me with their whole heart."[398] "In religion," says Thomas Watson, "the heart is all."[399]

---

[398] Jeremiah 24:7.
[399] Thomas Watson, *Discourses on Important Subjects*, Vol. I (Endinburgh: Blackie, Fullarton, & CO., 1829), 327.

We understand with the heart (Matt 13:15).

The word is sown in the heart (Matt 13:19).

The effects of the word depend on the state of the heart (Luke 8:10-15).

It is the heart that is blinded (Eph 4:18).

It is the heart that is opened (Acts 16:14)

It is the heart that must be changed by God's supernatural light, for it is the seat of our depravity and the fountain of all evil.[400] Evil, not only manifested in the practice of vile acts, but also in the performance of relatively virtuous acts, while the heart is far from God. "This people honoureth Me with their lips, but their heart is far from Me."[401] If these virtues exalt how good we appear in the eyes of men or make God indebted to us to reward our efforts and give us heaven, then we, like the Pharisees, will excel in them and give them a place of preeminence, all the while self still reigns supreme. Cyprian warned that those "whom Satan cannot prevail against by intemperance, those he prevails against by pride and vain glory."[402] If Satan cannot draw us away from God with the world (all these things I will give You if You will fall down and worship me), then he will temp us by transforming the world into our calling by adding "it is written."[403] Part of his craftiness involves using the very Word of God as a tool in his arsenal to tempt us away from the will of God. The apostle peter gives a prime example of this,

> As also in all his epistles, speaking in them of these
> things, in which are some things hard to understand,

---

[400] Mark 7:14 – 23.

[401] Mark 7:6.

[402] Tascius Caecilius Cyprian, from *A Body of Divinity*, Thomas Watson (Grand Rapids: Sovereign Grace Publishers; original, 1692), 8.

[403] Matthew 4:5 – 9.

which untaught and unstable people twist to their own
destruction, as they do also the other Scriptures.[404]

It is our willingness to say Amen to every word that proceeds from the
mouth of God that protects us from his devices. Those who give a hearty
amen to only a select few favorite portions of Scripture are defenseless.
The flesh is always seeking an easier route and a wider way. John Owen
explains,

> the world does not realize that gospel holiness deals
> with the heart and mind which no mortal eye can see
> and with which few are concerned. So gospel virtues are
> rejected in favor of those virtues which the world holds
> in high esteem.[405]

The truth is that the unregenerate can excel in outward observance.
But those who diligently seek God, seek Him with all their heart. It was
always the heart of man that God required. It is there where He sets up
his Kingdom to extend outward. Simply performing religious duties is
insufficient. Richard Baxter reveals why this is always the case:

> Truly, brethren, a man may as certainly, and more slyly,
> make haste to hell, in the way of earnest preaching of
> the gospel, and seeming zeal for a holy life, as in a way
> of drunkenness and filthiness. For what is holiness, but
> a devotedness to God and a living to Him? And what
> is a damnable state, but a devotedness to carnal self,
> and a living to ourselves? And doth anyone live more
> to himself, or less to God, than a proud man? And may
> not pride make a preacher study for himself and pray
> and preach, and live to himself, even when he seems to

---

[404] 2 Peter 3:16.

[405] John Owen, *Apostasy from the Gospel* (Carlisle: The Banner of Truth Trust,
2003), 115.

surpass others in the work? The work may be God's and yet we may do it, not for God, but for ourselves.[406]

Christ taught that those who have entered the Kingdom of God, have a righteousness that exceeds that of the Scribes and the Pharisees;[407] one that is not only outward and formal, but inward, vital, and of the heart. They study God's word because it is their delight. They pray because they take pleasure in communion with God. They do God's will because it is their meat and drink. This does not imply that they are completely without hypocrisy. But, unlike the Scribes and Pharisees, these outward exercises do not predominantly point to self. Therefore, a delight in self does not arise from their having engaged in them – "look how holy I am." In fact, the very opposite occurs. They delight in God and how great He is. And the clearer their view of God becomes, the smaller their service for Him appears in their own eyes. The very boasting of the Pharisees before God about their fasting and tithes[408] proves that their heart was unchanged. Their satisfaction with mere outward observance alone shows that God was never their aim. Their religion was a mere commodity to be consumed on self, driven by the need for esteem, whether from God or man, that they believed the outward observance could generate.

As Antinomianism is not the result of taking the gospel too far, but not taking it far enough, so, Legalism is not the result of taking the law too far, but the result of not taking it far enough. The problem with the Pharisees was not that their righteousness was too strict, but that it was not strict enough. They lowered the extent of God's commands to their own natural ability. They sought merely to clean the outside of the cup, while their hearts were full of wickedness.[409] They sought to impress God by adhering only to the outward letter of the law, while overlooking the most important part of the law; the very spirit and aim of the law itself. Christ calls them foolish for supposing that He who has the right to command the outer, does not have the right to command the inner. All who likewise

---

[406] Richard Baxter, *The Reformed Pastor*r (Glasgow: William Collins, 1835; original, 1656), 217.

[407] Matthew 5:20.

[408] Luke 18:10 – 14.

[409] Luke 11:39 – 44.

clean up the outer life, while ignoring or lessening the importance of the heart, are likewise foolish in the eyes of Christ. John Flavel said,

> It is a cheap and easy way to give God the external service and worship of the body, but heart work is hard work.[410]

Gardinar Spring explains why such work is both cheap and easy,

> For as he thinketh in his heart, so is he (Prov 23:7). The moral quality of actions lies in the disposition of heart with which they are performed. . .Mere morality never aims at the heart and would never touch it if it should. It may lop off the luxuriances of human depravity, but it never strikes at the root.....However fair this exterior, and however accordant with the expectations of the world, it falls far short of what a man must be to become either holy or happy.[411]

The Pharisees had wrong views about what God requires, because they had wrong views about who God is. Their God was too small. That's why they could draw near to Him with a high view of themselves and their accomplishments, while the tax collector had come to realize the greatness of God and his own corresponding sinfulness.[412] The true knowledge of God humbles man as it exalts God. Since God is so infinitely glorious, all the service that we could possibly render onto Him must be far below His infinite worth. We have no evidence that we have come to perceive His perfections, unless we have also come to perceive our own imperfections, and the inadequacy of all our works to impress Him in any way. He must be a small god indeed who is impressed by any of our works. This is why

---

[410] John Flavel, *The Works of Rev. John Flavel*, Vol. IV (London: J Mathews, 1799), 281.

[411] Gardinar Spring, *The Distinguishing Traits of Christian Character* (Philadelphia: Presbyterian and Reformed Publishing Co., 1972; original 1853), 9.

[412] Luke 18:9 – 14.

William Beveridge would say, "Not only the worst of my sins, but the best of my duties speak me a child of Adam."[413]

While we should never repent for having performed good works, we should always repent of them that they were no better. The only reason we think our half-hearted service is worthy of Him is because we have low views of His majesty and high views of ourselves. This is not to say that our service will not be accepted and rewarded, if done, however imperfectly, by faith, according to His Word, and for His glory. But we must recognize that apart from Christ these works would be nothing but an abomination in the sight of such a holy Being. All who think otherwise have misunderstood His exalted nature, and could not have been allured to a religious life by the brightness of His glory, but by the prospects of their own potential religious glory. They thus continue to work only for themselves, rather than God, for their salvation, rewards, reputation or temporal blessings. God has determined to reward us according to our service, not because these works are good in themselves, but because He has determined to regard them as such in Christ Jesus. And any rewards for such service are not the reward of merit, but of grace. The glory of God is thereby increased, while the glory of man is eliminated. We will receive the crown, for we have truly acted. But God will receive the honor, for we have only been acted upon, and He has acted on our behalf on the cross. Therefore, even these crowns must be laid at His feet. Humility, not pride, should be the only response for all that we accomplish by His grace and for His glory; otherwise, we plainly show that what was done was not done by His grace nor for His glory.

The greater God is in your eyes, the lower you will view yourself and your service, and the greater you will be viewed by God. For the tax collector received that which the Pharisee could not. He walked away justified.[414] "But on this one will I look; on him who is poor and of a contrite spirit, and who trembles at My Word."[415] God's thoughts toward

---

[413] William Bereridge, from *The Treasury of David*, C H Spurgeon (New York: Funk and Wagnalls, 1886), 314.

[414] Luke 18:14.

[415] Isaiah 66:2.

us are directly contrary to the thoughts we have of ourselves.[416] Robert Bolton says,

> the more vile any man is in his own eyes the more precious he is in God's.[417]

Listen also to the words of Augustus Montague Toplandy,

> The sweetest seasons on this side of heaven are, when the soul sinks as into nothing before the face of God, and is absorbed in the sight of Christ and the love of the Spirit; when we feel the presence of Deity, and silently wait on Him, at the foot of the cross, with weeping eyes, melting affections, and bleeding hearts.[418]

Self-abasement is not an unusual frame of mind of a few Christians. It is the highest place that we can stand before God, for it is the only proper expression of faith in the greatness of the God before whom we stand. It is not only experienced at the beginning of the Christian life, but throughout the Christian life. Spiritual growth does not abate it, but rather increases it. Self-abasement is totally consistent with that confidence by which we "come boldly unto the throne of grace."[419] For this confidence is the fruit of faith in His finished work, rather than anything that we have done. The stronger the faith in Christ's finished work, the stronger this confidence in God grows, in opposition to that confidence in the flesh which approaches God on the merit of one's own achievement. Thomas Manton says,

> The more true light a man hath, the more cause of self-abasement will he find in himself. You can never debase self enough; and certainly Christ is more exalted when

---

[416] Revelation 3:17.

[417] Robert Bolton, *The Carnal Professor* (Ligonier: Soli Deo Gloria Publications, 1992; original, 1634), 48.

[418] Augustus Montague Toplady, *The Works of Augustus M. Toplady* (London: Williams Baynes, 1825), 263.

[419] Hebrews 4:16.

we are most abased (Is 2:19). If Christ shall be precious
to you, you must be vile in your own eyes.[420]

Hugh Binning confirms the same when he writes,

> But as the water that comes from a height, the lower
> it comes down the higher it ascends up again; so the
> humble spirit, the lower it falls in its own estimation,
> the higher it is raised in real worth and in God's
> estimation.[421]

Satan will allow men to abound in doing that which is good in a relative
sense, if it will produce that which is evil in an absolute sense (pride). He
thereby renders the doing of that which is truly good impossible. He is
more than willing to allow men to subdue their passions and overcome
sensual wickedness, if he can ruin them by their pride, which is spiritual
wickedness. He transforms his ministers into ministers of righteousness;[422]
his wolves into sheep, outwardly.[423] He can effect an outward change
without the inner. The Pharisees were very religious, yet Christ calls them
"of your father the devil."[424] Paul, before his conversion, was outwardly
blameless,[425] yet lost. The encounter of Jesus with the rich young ruler
proves that it is possible to live a moral life, have a desire for heaven, and yet
remain unconverted.[426] Even evil doers can do many apparent wonderful
things in Christ's name[427] with the full expectation of being rewarded for
their efforts.

There are many ways that self can use God, or the things of God, for

---

[420] Thomas Manton, *Commentary on Jude* (Grand Rapids: Kregel Publications,
1988; original, 1658), 46.

[421] Hugh Binning, *The Works of the Rev. Hugh Binning* (Ligonier: Soli Deo
Gloria, 1992), 545.

[422] 2 Corinthians 11:13 – 15.

[423] Matthew 7:16.

[424] John 8:44.

[425] Philippians 3:6.

[426] Luke 18:21 – 23.

[427] Matthew 7:21 – 23.

its own ends. William Romaine even describes how easy one can pursue self under a cloak of holiness:

> When He hath brought us low, we do not like to be kept there, we want to get up again: our foolish desire is, that He may do something in us for which we may have a good opinion of ourselves; and so with this thought we are apt to wish, O that I were more holy! O that I could pray better! O that I was more spiritual in duties! O that I was thankful enough! If you could come to the true nature of these wishes (specious as they appear), you would find them spring from the secret workings of a proud, self-righteous spirit; take off their cloak of holiness, and their meaning is this, 'I wish God would give me something for which I might be pleased with myself.' If this is the case, would not the eye be turned inward upon this very good self, and be drawn off from looking unto Jesus? And so far as self is something, Christ is made nothing.[428]

As the worldly man seeks distinction in the world for his wealth, talent, beauty, position, and learning, the hypocrite seeks to excel those in the church with those things that the church holds in high esteem. If he cannot excel others in gifts and learning, he will do so in a show of humility or holiness. If he cannot be distinguished for his wisdom and leadership, he will be so for his service and giving. He approaches the church much like a market, using his outward observance, learning, or leadership qualities to purchase for himself the respect, esteem, and approval he believes he deserves from others. It is not uncommon for such men, whose goal is to have all men think well of their religion, to become overly zealous in the performance of the externals of religion, while neglecting the religion of the heart. Many mistake the outward for the inward, and falsely believe they are Christians. But the outward is performed solely for the reputation that it gives and the attention that is

---

[428] William Romaine, *Letters from the Late Rev. William Romaine, A. M* (London: Smith and Elder, 1822), 269.

draws to self. They seek not God, but themselves as their primary object. "A good name is rather to be chosen than great riches,"[429] they say, and so begin to pursue it as a legitimate end. But a good name is not the ultimate end, it is the by-product of a life lived by that wisdom which both begins and ends with the fear of the Lord,[430] and not the fear of what others may think of us. The deceitfulness of hypocrisy is that it makes that which is perfectly legitimate and compatible with a religious life to reflect upon oneself as the primary object, rather than a means of exalting the most excellent Object.

God finds the sin of hypocrisy utterly repulsive,[431] for He does not look at the outward act so much as the secrets of the heart.[432] He desires that we be holy in heart, and not merely in external actions.[433] Hypocrisy is defined as any change of behavior, without a change of heart. The goal of hypocrisy is the exaltation of self; therefore, it is the rejection of God for the idol of self. It is the effect of self-love. And unless we take away the cause, the effects will not cease. David Tappan describes the process,

> This enmity can be removed only by the removal of its cause: which is accomplished when we become radically changed and renewed from sinful idolatry, by the Spirit of the divine Redeemer. When this is effected, we are reconciled to God; being now conformed in disposition to His moral character.[434]

Our hearts must first be turned from self, before our eyes can be turned from self. If the cause were removed by the implanting of a true saving knowledge, hypocrisy, which is the fruit of ignorance and unbelief, would cease.

If we would but consider who He is, it would draw off our attention from the baser objects of the world, including the praise of men. For in

---

[429] Proverbs 22:1.

[430] Psalm 111:10; Ecclesiastes 12:13.

[431] Isaiah 1:11 – 15.

[432] Matthew 5:28.

[433] Matthew 5:8; Ezekiel 33:30 – 32.

[434] David Tappan, *Sermons on Important Subjects by the Late Rev. David Tappan* (Boston: W. Hilliard and Lincoln & Edmand, 1807), 161.

light of who He is, what are all the kingdoms of this world that they should draw our attention? And what an insignificant thing is the opinion of man. This is the true test and task of the ministers of God; to show how great God is, and, by way of contrast, the smallness of everything else. If they fail at this task, they only promote hypocrisy, proving their ignorance both of God's greatness and man's smallness. Thus, they become the most effectual instruments in the hands of Satan himself, whose kingdom is promoted by "blinding the minds of them which believe not." Whereas, the true servants of God promote His Kingdom by "making manifest the savour of His knowledge," and not their own. "For we preach not ourselves, but Christ Jesus the Lord; and ourselves your servants for Jesus' sake."[435]

---

[435] 2 Corinthians 4:5.

CHAPTER 11

The Saving Knowledge of God – Its Source and Object

For God, who commanded the light to shine out of darkness, hath shined in our hearts, to give the light of the knowledge of the glory of God in the face of Jesus Christ

1 Corinthians 4:6

Its Source and Object: God, "to give the light of the knowledge of the glory of God."

None can be drawn by the alluring brightness of His glory, who have no knowledge of that glory. This knowledge is not merely the result of intellectual endeavor. For such endeavors are always ineffectual until God shines His light upon the heart through the Spirit. One glimpse of the glory of God does more to enlighten the soul than all speculative knowledge of scripture apart from this grace. It is only the divine influence that makes such knowledge effectual.[436]

God gives us a heart to know Him (Jer 24:7).

---

[436] Acts 16:14.

> It is God who gives us a heart to perceive, eyes to see and ears to hear (Deut 29:4).

> Christ gives light (Eph 5:14).

> Christ is the light (John 11:46).

God not only "shines in our hearts", but the light that He shines is the knowledge of Himself. He becomes at once both Object and Source. Christ gives light, because He is light. The light that He gives is the knowledge of Himself. This means that we are not to look for some inner light within us; on the contrary, we are to look away from self, and unto Christ, the Source and Object of light. If any should inquire as to whether or not he has experienced this light, he must judge the reality of the cause only by its effects, and not by any feeling or experience, however moving. Satan can counterfeit any of the feelings and experiences of the godly. But the effect of all that he causes, unlike the illuminating work of the Spirit, does not lead to the glorification of Christ,[437] but to the gratification of some aspect of the flesh. To cherish the counterfeit offers of a consumer-driven Christianity, then, is always to cherish our corruptions. Satan does not always steal the word sown in our hearts, he oftentimes allows us to receive it with joy, so long as the root of the matter is not found in us. He does not mind our service, prayers, giving and searching of the Scripture, so long as these are the effects of self-love and not for the promotion of God's glory, which glory he has coveted since before the creation of man.

All the operations of the Spirit are like the wind.[438] While we cannot see the wind, we do see its effects. "So is every one that is born of the Spirit." All our actions, experiences, religious feelings, and knowledge, that have the Spirit as its cause, will generate three particular effects:

First, it will show men how blind and helpless they are. It will give them a knowledge of themselves.[439] A true saving view of the glory of God, at first, is always accompanied with a sense of His wrath and displeasure,

---

[437] John 16:14 – 15.
[438] John 3:8.
[439] Isaiah 6:5.

"For all have sinned, and come short of the glory of God."[440] We will not go to the source from whence a new heart proceeds, unless we first see that "the heart is deceitful above all things and desperately wicked;"[441] and that it is "from within, out of the heart of men," that evil proceeds.[442] Unless we see the heart as the source of all evil, we will not see it as the proper subject of grace, and settle for a mere superficial change.

A deceitful heart, in order to continually depend upon itself, must smooth over sin, and present it as something other than its true colors. It "heals the wounds of these people slightly."[443] Self has not yet been fully unmasked if we still depend upon it. All such self-dependence is highly offensive to the One upon whom all things depend. When we view ourselves too highly, we do not view Him correctly. We are void of all spiritual sight, unless we see ourselves as nothing in our own eyes. We must first distrust ourselves if we are to trust Him. Self-dependence sets up self above Him, and it is proof that He is not the exalted Object before our eyes, but merely ourselves. None can look upon the sun without losing sight of everything else.

Secondly, the proper knowledge of God gives us the true value of everything else. Our eyes have not seen the gloriousness of God unless we find the glory of the world utterly worthless. What the church offers reveals its values. What it values reveals its objects of worship. To lure with the world implies that one is still of the world; that one is still following the course of the world.[444] So long as the church insists on presenting to the world its own idols, it reveals its own idolatry.[445] Idolatry is the fruit of believing that some created object is more important than God; that this world is more important than the one to come. It is acting as if this world was all. The idolatry in our hearts will never be brought down until the true knowledge of God is set up. Self-love will never be made subordinate until we get a glimpse, by divine grace, of something far lovelier. Christ

---

[440] Romans 3:23.

[441] Jeremiah 17:9.

[442] Mark 7:21.

[443] Jeremiah 6:14, 8:11.

[444] Ephesians 2:2.

[445] "Let us through grace labour to see the excellency of spiritual things, and how cheap and poor must all the glory of the world appear!" Richard Sibbes. *Divine Meditations*, 147.

died to deliver us from the world. And none can consider himself delivered from the world, who do not see its vanity.

The true knowledge of God is all-exclusive. It overthrows all the idols of the heart, including the idol of self. To know Him truly and intelligently while idolizing anything else is an impossibility. To profess to know Christ, who was self-sacrificing, meek, lowly, forgiving, and always seeking the will of the Father, while remaining self-serving, consumed with our own plans, unforgiving, prideful and self-focused, is to be grossly ignorant of the very Object of this knowledge, and is the surest evidence of spiritual blindness. And how does God heal this blindness? According to Solomon Stoddard,

> The way wherein God communicates grace is by teaching men how glorious He is. He lets in gospel light and so works gracious inclinations. Men see the reason why they should love God, trust in Christ, and be humble, and this inclines the heart that way.....At the same time that they see reason to exalt God, they see the evil of pride. When they see reason to love God, they see that there is no reason to dote on the world.... When love to God is put into the soul, inordinate self-love is mortified.[446]

The third effect of that light which has God both as its source and its object is the reverence and worship of God. This is clearly seen every time God manifests His presence throughout the Scriptures.[447] If you have been given any spiritual light at all, it is the light of the knowledge of the glory of God. This glorious knowledge puts an end to all our glorying in lesser things. The prophet Jeremiah writes,

> Let not the wise man glory in his wisdom, neither let the mighty man glory in his might, let not the rich man

---

[446] Solomon Stoddard, *The Nature of Saving Conversion* (Morgan: Soli Deo Gloria Publications, 1999; original, 1719), 22 – 23.

[447] Joshua 5:14, Ezekiel 1:28, Daniel 8:17 – 18, Revelation 1:17.

glory in his riches: but let him that glorieth glory in this,
that he understandeth and knoweth Me.[448]

Once this higher glory has appeared, to glory in anything less,
whether wisdom, riches or power, is to glory in our shame.[449] However
glorious these things may appear to unenlightened man, those spiritually
illuminated have received new sight. Thus, those whose priority in religion
is, "What's in it for me?" are spiritually blind. The consumer-driven
church, therefore, by grasping for those things that an unenlightened
world seeks, proves that it has nothing more in its hands to offer the world
than the same empty offers of an unenlightened world. Ironically, the more
these counterfeit offers are utilized to attract the unenlightened, the less
enlightened they become.[450]

Since God is such an exalted Being, the only evidence that He has
revealed Himself to us is the continual exaltation of Him in our lives. We
cannot truly behold the exalted One without exalting Him. The Object of
divine illumination is so all-surpassingly lovely and glorious that it draws
the affections of all those who are its recipients to reach out to Him with
awe and love. And this is always the order. If you love a god who does not
awe you, then you love an idol. If all that you find amazing about God is
His grace, then you are still a graceless wretch. Love, if it has God as its
object, does not merely acknowledge His character, but is profoundly in
awe of Him, and willingly responds in worship. Once the affections are
drawn to love, the will is inclined to choose. It is only then that we can
be said to truly know Him. For it is only from a proper view of God's
character that love arises. Love that arises without awe does not perceive
God's character correctly. This is the surest way to distinguish between
the conversion of the heart, and one merely of the head.

None can love any object unless they first see its loveliness. Perceiving
loveliness presupposes love, or else we would perceive no loveliness. Once
the eyes of our understanding are opened to see the excellencies of God's
perfections, we cannot but love Him on account of them. For the same
operations of the Spirit that opens the eyes of the understanding, also

---

[448] Jeremiah 9:24.
[449] Philippians 3:19.
[450] Matthew 23:15.

enlarges the heart. It is from this spiritual beholding of God by faith, in all His perfections, that all that is truly spiritual in our thoughts and actions proceed, and ultimately find acceptance with Him. The hypocrite may have many of the same outward actions as the child of God, but these actions are void of any spiritual significance, since they do not spring from this spiritual principle of love. And the principle of love cannot exist apart from the knowledge of the Beloved. "The exercise of love is always in proportion to the degree of our sense of the divine beauty,"[451] says Joseph Bellamy.

All of our boasting about knowing God is a lie, if it does not produce these three effects. All so called love for God that does not have Him as its supreme Object, cannot have Him as its source; therefore, it is not a saving knowledge. This means that all those who love God, or the things of God, mainly as they reflect upon the object of self, cannot be saved. For the love of God above oneself, which is what the true knowledge of God requires, causes one to deny himself; yea, and by comparison even to hate his own life. Richard Baxter said that "Christ cannot be the Way, where the creature is the end."[452] Therefore, consumer-driven Christianity, by placing the customer first, and offering him all those things that self seeks, cannot be the way to God, but merely an alternative way to self. Whenever self is our end, we do not intend to show them God in all His loveliness, desirableness and fearfulness; rather, we will only want to show them ourselves in all of our talent, eloquence and wit. Since, we assume, they will not find God sufficiently lovely to attract them unto Himself, we, like Absalom by the city gate,[453] proceed to show them how relevant and wonderful we are to attract them unto ourselves.

That which is the object of faith for the individual Christian, should be the supreme object of the church collectively. Sadly, the church of today would rather boast of their wisdom, power, and material wealth, than in the highest honor of knowing God.[454] And this only proves that the

---

[451] Joseph Bellamy, *Sin, the Law, and the Gospel* (Ames: International Outreach, 1998), 148.

[452] Richard Baxter, *The Saint's Everlasting Rest* (New York: American Tract Society), 105.

[453] 2 Samuel 15:2 – 6.

[454] Jeremiah 9:23 – 24.

saving knowledge of God is lacking. Much of what passes for worship in some churches is idolatry, because its first consideration is not God, but man. It exists to impress man and produce pleasant feelings within him, thereby making church both an impressive and pleasant thing of which to be a part. When our concern is to arrange the church's worship to the liking of our customers, our goal is not to obey God, but to perform before men. And when man becomes the audience, he also becomes the object of worship. So long as we are bowed before them, we cannot lead them in the worship of God, but only to follow us in the worship of themselves, for our catering to their desires and felt-needs reinforces their idolatrous false assessment of themselves.

We worship idols when we exalt anything to the place that rightfully belongs to God alone. We worship God, on the other hand, by placing everything second to Him. The church must recognize that corporal worship is not a form of entertainment for man, but the public act of glorifying who God is from the heart, and a thankfulness for all He has done.[455] To the extent that it depends upon (or is impressed with) technology, talent, size or personalities, its focus is turned from God. True worship is not concerned with impressing people, but with exalting God. Its focus is not to fill the church with more and more people, while revealing less and less of who God really is and what He really requires. Its primary goal is not to be uplifting to man, but to lift up God and bring Him glory. The direct result of this will be uplifting to man only because we can lift man no higher in our ministry than by directing him toward fulfilling the original purpose of his creation, bringing glory to God. This means that we are to come away from worship not asking, "was I edified?", but "was God glorified?"; not whether the worship arts were successful in securing the attention of man, but whether these were successful in directing our attention to God and away from human talent. And to the extent that these arts were directed toward us, God finds them as unacceptable as the religious show of the Pharisees. For all worship that is Spirit empowered is always directed toward Christ.

In the case of unbelievers, however, the goal of our public gatherings should not be to lift up man, but to reveal God. Our job, then, is to

---

[455] Romans 1:21.

preach Christ,[456] and not partially, but as Lord. Doing this will bring more conviction than comfort at first. The apostle Paul explains,

> But if all prophesy, and there come in one that believeth not, or one unlearned, he is convinced of all, he is judged of all; And thus are the secrets of his heart made manifest; and so falling down on his face he will worship God, and report that God is in you of a truth.[457]

Let us not be detoured from revealing our God simply because certain aspects of His nature might offend some. As much as we try to win men into our fellowship by our smooth talk, unless they fall down on their face in worship before God, they are still idol worshipers headed for eternal destruction. We do no favor to those who are headed toward eternal destruction by enticing them to attend our church with those things that are likewise headed toward eternal destruction, such as popularity, eloquence, charismatic personalities, political influence, amusing programs or human wisdom. Faith that rests on man's personality, eloquence or wisdom,[458] worships man's personality, eloquence and wisdom, and empties the cross of its power.[459] A Faith that rests on Christ, joins the church because Christ is lifted up, even when men preach Him in "weakness", "fear and much trembling", and without "persuasive words of human wisdom;"[460] even when it is not the popular thing to do.

If it is true, as many affirm, that theology is for doxology, then it must be equally true that our doxology reveals our theology. If our worship is man-centered, then it must be because we have first embraced a theology that has a deficient view of the glory of God. The goal, then, is not to promote just any worship, but biblical worship. There is no lack of worship in the world, for all men worship something. Even among those who profess to worship God, there are many who worship what they know

---

[456] Philippians 1:18, Colossians 1:28.
[457] 1 Corinthians 14:24 – 25.
[458] 1 Corinthians 2:4 – 5.
[459] 1 Corinthians 1:17.
[460] 1 Corinthians 2:2 – 4.

not.[461] If our worship does not inspire reverence and awe,[462] then we can be sure that we do not promote the worship of God, but a less threatening golden calf that we have tailor-made to suit the whims of the multitude. True worship requires that our concept of God, as well as the outward expression of that inward conception, be both biblical and spiritual;[463] done not only according to the prescription of God's Word (the truth), but from the spiritual principle of sincere love (in truth), the spiritual end of God's glory, and in a spiritual manner (with all our heart, soul, mind and strength).

Worship that is God-centered leaves no room for consumer-friendly worship, which breaks all the above principles. Consumer-friendly worship, by nature, is always centered on self, whether in regard to its manner or its matter; that is, either performed in such a manner that accord with one's fallen desires or toward an object that accords with these desires. Any crowd would enthusiastically praise a messiah who would fulfill their desire for freedom from Roman bondage. Thus, they cried out "Hosanna, Hosanna" not with any regard for the person of Christ, but for the services that they thought the messiah would render on their behalf.

Exuberant outward expression may result from beholding Christ by faith in all His glory, but when exuberant outward expression becomes the goal, rather than spiritually beholding Christ, it is excitement for excitement sake. When we lose a sense of the awe of God, we have lost sight of His glory, and have become susceptible to be awed by the lesser glories that center on ourselves. Like the before mentioned Jews, we also worship a false messiah if we desire a Christianity that promises to wipe our slate of sin clean, while leaving us to freely continue to live in them. This is not a worship that reflects God's glory, but one that reflects a lesser glory – ourselves, and is therefore irrational. Reasonable worship lays down the whole life in the service of God.[464] And what characterizes this life is its nonconformity to the world[465] and humility.[466] In the Scriptures, the

---

461 John 4:22.

462 Hebrews 12:28.

463 John 4:23.

464 Romans 12:1.

465 Romans 12:2.

466 Romans 12:3.

immediate affect of a sense of the Divine presence was not exuberant self-expression, but fear, awe and self-abasement.[467]

Finally, we must not only recognize that acceptable worship is an expression of the whole life as it extends God-ward, but also that the life that extends towards God in worship will likewise extend outward towards people in good works. This is not to be confused with the social gospel, which dishonors God by making His worship to consist primarily in its service and benefit to others. The true gospel is serviceable to man only in that it seeks to honor God by reflecting His good nature towards all men. Good works do not end in the good done to man, but reflect the good nature of the God we serve. It is in this way that they perform the highest service to man. Only God is to be loved with all our heart. When we love man, it must only be with a subordinate love – as we love ourselves. We cannot make the nature of true religion, as some do, consist only in the love of man any more than we can make it consist, as others do, in the love of ourselves. While it is true that all our religion is in vain without it,[468] all expressions of love to man must be God-centered. "That they may see your good works, and glorify your Father which is in heaven."[469] "By this we know that we love the children of God, when we love God, and keep His commandments."[470]

True worship incorporates all of life's responsibilities into the service of God, therefore Christ teaches,

> Therefore if thou bring thy gift to the alter, and there rememberest that thy brother hath ought against thee; leave there thy gift before the altar, and go thy way; first be reconciled to thy brother, and then come and offer thy gift.[471]

The author of Hebrews also exhorts us,

---

[467] Isaiah 6:1 – 5; Job 42:5,6; Genesis 28:16,17.
[468] James 1:27.
[469] Matthew 5:16.
[470] 1 John 5:2.
[471] Matthew 5:23 – 24.

By him therefore let us offer the sacrifice of praise to God continually, that is, the fruit of our lips giving thanks to his name. But to do good and to communicate forget not; for with such sacrifices God is well pleased.[472]

And Jeremiah reveals the true knowledge of God when he writes,

He judged the cause of the poor and needy; then it was well with him: was not this to know Me? saith the Lord.[473]

Gregory the Great illustrated this biblical concept quite well,

As the boat cannot move rightly when the oars only on one side are plied; or as the fowl, if she use only one wing, cannot fly up: so religion consisteth of duties to be performed, some to God and some to man; some for the first table of the law, some for the second; otherwise that religion will never profit that hath one hand wrapped up that should be towards man in all offices of charity, through the other be used towards God in all offices of piety.[474]

Like Christ, he is not merely suggesting that we incorporate benevolence into our life of worship that up until now has been lacking. He is expressing the utter lack of acceptable worship without it. No matter how great an outward show, or how loud a "sounding brass or tinkling cymbal," we are not true worshippers without it.

---

[472] Hebrews 13:15 – 16.

[473] Jeremiah 22:16.

[474] Gregory the Great, from *A Homiletic Encyclopedia* (New York: Funk and Wagnalls, 1885), 699.

CHAPTER 12

The Saving Knowledge Of God – Its Consequences

But we all, with open face, beholding as in a glass the glory of the Lord, are changed into the same image from glory to glory, even as by the Spirit of the Lord.

2 Corinthians 3:18

Its Consequences: Practical Holiness, "are changed into the same image"

It is a transforming knowledge. Although we have not been enlightened perfectly, we have been enlightened to shine; "Let your light so shine."[475] The believer does not only behold the glory of the Lord, he also reflects it. As Moses' face shown with the glory it beheld in God, we too are to reflect the Lord's glory with lives that are transformed more and more into His likeness.[476] The best indication of our approach unto God, is a life that conforms to Him; and the nearer the approach, the greater the resemblance of His likeness shines forth from our lives. How much, or how little, we behold the glory of the Lord, will determine how much, or how little, we reflect that image in our lives. And how much, or how little, we reflect His likeness reveals how much, or how little, we behold His glory.

---

[475] Matthew 5:16.
[476] 2 Corinthians 3:9 – 18.

> The knowledge of the Lord is a practical knowledge
> (James 3:13 – 18).
>
> It is a moral knowledge (Jer 22:15 – 17).
>
> The Lord opens the heart to heed (Acts 16:14).
>
> Those who are taught by Christ are taught to put off the
> old man and put on the new, according to God (Eph
> 4:20 – 24).

To speak of the practical implications of the work of God on the soul in effecting holy practice could make some in the church uncomfortable, and this would conflict with the goal of creating a non-threatening atmosphere within the church that is welcoming to all and offensive to none. When nominal Christianity becomes prevalent, those who seek to attract the masses must invent a theology that accommodates nominal Christianity. But this very goal proves that it is not the knowledge of God that we promote, but merely a comfortable environment that would attract and retain those who desire only a superficial knowledge of God that quiets the conscience and affords peace of mind, while men continue to live as they please. Our means always corresponds with our ends. If we set the glory of God as our end, this would dictate the path of our ministry to the world. But if we misjudge the end, we will likewise mistake the means. Therefore, theological accommodation to man is the only possible outcome of establishing man as the end.

Contextualization, while necessary to our mission to reach the world, does not extend to our worship of God. This worship is only prescribed in the Scriptures, and is not dictated by culture, especially if it is a culture that is "all about me." In Christ's mission to rescue us, He became one of us, and found no area of society off limits to His ministry. In this mission, we find Him with publicans, tax collectors and even those living in adultery; at feasts, weddings and suppers. But once inside the Temple, however, He quickly began to cleanse it and continually confronted those who were the regulators of its outward worship for their abuses and hypocrisy. Things that were not confronted outside, could not be tolerated within. While the city of God is to intermingle with the city of man, the city of man must never have influence over the city of God. The church, being the called-out ones, must maintain a separation, not from the people of the world, but the principles that motivate those in the world. The bride of Christ must never defile herself by allowing the practices of society to influence her corporate or individual expression of devotion to Him.

"Holy practice," says Edwards, "is as much the end of all that God does about His saints, as fruit is the end of all the husbandman does about the growth of his field or vineyard; as the matter is often represented in Scripture, Matt. iii. 10, chapter xiii. 8, 23, 30-38, chapter xxi. 19, 33, 34, Luke xiii. 6, John xv. 1-8, 1 Cor. iii. 9, Heb. vi. 7,8, Isa. v. 1-8, Cant. viii. 11,12, Isa. xxvii. 2,3. And therefore everything in a true Christian is calculated to reach this end. This fruit of holy practice is what every grace, and every discovery, and every individual thing which belongs to Christian experience, has a direct tendency to."[477] Thomas Scott also believed that there could be no saving knowledge without this transformation into holiness. He said,

> This transformation of the soul into conformity to Christ is the proper evidence and test of spiritual illumination; without a measure of it, all supposed discoveries and revelations are mere delusions and enthusiasm.[478]

John Flavel adds,

> All the discoveries God makes to us of Himself in Christ have an assimilating quality, and change the soul into their own likeness.[479]

Having shown in the previous chapter that the worship of God is the proper effect of "the knowledge of the glory of God", it is important to establish the further fact that conformity to that knowledge will follow.

---

[477] Edwards, *Works*, Vol. III, 291.

[478] Thomas Scott, *Scott's Family Bible* (Philadelphia: William W. Woodward, 1818), 2 Corinthians 3:18.

[479] John Flavel, *The Method of Grace* (New York: American Tract Society, first American edition), 387.

Becoming God's children does not allow us free reign to serve our old idols. Those who profess to cherish Him above all else, while in practice permitting themselves to prefer their former idols, despise Him, rather than worship Him. The true desire to cherish the preeminence of Christ will be reflected in our practice. Those who too easily cleave to themselves are just as easily prone to forsake God. Without the work of His Spirit upon our hearts to dethrone these idols, we will never truly labor for the glory of God, nor the good of man.

Worship always terminates in a life of conformity to the object of worship. We cannot worship Him for His attributes without esteeming those attributes worthy of our imitation. His attributes have no value to us at all if we do not endeavor to possess them, for we always desire to possess that which we highly esteem. Therefore, there can be no adoration without assimilation.

To profess admiration for His person, while ignoring His desires expressed in His Word, is self-deception. We really do not esteem Him as a Sovereign, and our inattentiveness to His Word is an insult to His sovereignty. We cannot worship the sovereign God appropriately, while remaining unwilling to surrender to His sovereignty. Such worship would only be a mockery of His sovereignty. All of our so-called worship is nothing but an affront, unless we bring with it a life of corresponding action. When worship truly flows from the heart, it will extend to the life, and not just a part of the life, but the whole of it. How can we esteem Him in our hearts, if we do not imitate and obey Him with our lives? By this decisive factor we distinguish true saving knowledge from all that is counterfeit:

> And hereby we do know that we know Him, if we keep
> His commandments. He that saith, I know Him, and
> keepeth not His commandments, is a liar, and the truth
> is not in him.[480]

A true desire to worship God is inseparable from a true desire for holiness, and therefore it is inseparable from a life of holiness. Unless we behold the glory of His holiness, we cannot perceive the glory of His other

---

[480] 1 John 2:3 – 4.

attributes. His holiness is not one among many attributes, it is the totality of all of His attributes. In fact, it is not an attribute at all. It is the crown that holds together all the jewels of His attributes in place. Remove the crown and all the others are removed.

> "The more frequently he beholds Him, the more fully he knows His perfections of which His holiness is the ornament. The more he knows them, the more ardently he loves them. The more he loves them, the more he desires a conformity to them; for love aspires after a likeness to the beloved."[481]
>
> Abraham Booth

> "A person of real holiness is much affected and taken up in the admiration of the holiness of God. Unholy persons may be somewhat affected and taken with the other excellences of God.... it is only holy souls that are taken and affected with His holiness. The more holy any are, the more deeply are they affected by this....To the holy angels, the holiness of God is the sparking diamond in the ring of glory. But unholy persons are affected and taken with anything rather than this."[482]
>
> Thomas Brooks

While God is rich in mercy and mighty in power, He is glorious in holiness.[483] When our eyes are more turned toward our own glory, we will shy away from this attribute and begin to exalt some of the others. To worship Him for His mercy and love toward us, to praise Him for His work of redemption on the cross for us, and to rejoice in all the benefits that flow from that work, is consistent with self-love, unless we first and foremost worship Him for His majestic holiness. "A true love for God

---

[481] Abraham Booth, *The Reign of Grace* (New York: Robert Carter, 1851), 208.

[482] Thomas Brooks, *The Complete Works of Thomas Brooks*, Vol. IV (Edinburgh: James Nichol, 1867), 104.

[483] Exodus 15:11.

must begin with a delight in His Holiness,"[484] says Edwards. His majesty deserves our worship whether we are benefited or not. It is only when we are so awe struck by His holiness that we can praise Him correctly for all His benefits, for only then will He remain the focus and not ourselves.

Although God's glory cannot be known in its essence, enough of that glory must be known, so as to draw off our affections from the world, ourselves and everything else that might compete with that glory. Enough must be cherished in the heart to impede our wandering from Him. Otherwise, we will only come to Him with our own preeminence in view, and so be drawn to Him solely for our own benefit; our own safety will be all that secures our attachment to Him and inhibit our wandering from Him. When we merely desire the fruit of religion, despite all of our outward show, we disobey His command to "have no other gods before Me."[485] "To pretend a homage to God, and intend only the advantage of self, is rather to mock Him than to worship Him," says Stephen Charnock.[486]

While His glorious perfections are the foundation of worship, the view of God's mercies (Christ's death on the cross and all the benefits that flow from it) are nevertheless, powerful motivations, not only for the worship of our lips, but also for the sacrifice of our life, which is the only reasonable worship.[487] Anything short of a complete sacrifice of ourselves is unreasonable. And those who promote the religion of self have never truly thought things out. Should not He who paid for our redemption with His blood deserve our total devotion? Yes, He would deserve it even if He had not redeemed us. But in light of His sacrifice on our behalf, would it not be the most ungrateful act to regard our time, money, or all of our life as too precious to be totally devoted to Him?

God's love, as well as His holiness, should be highly esteemed, especially since we did nothing to deserve His love, but rather deserved the contrary. This love is only properly esteemed, not by producing thoughts of

---

[484] Jonathan Edwards, *The Religious Affections* (Carlisle: Banner of Truth Trust, 1997; original, 1746), 183.

[485] Exodus 20:3.

[486] Stephen Charnock, *Discourses upon the Existence and Attributes of God* (London: Thomas Tegg, 1840, reprint), 149,150.

[487] Romans 12:1.

our own self-importance, but by producing gratitude, which manifests in a life of self-sacrifice. This gratitude continues only so long as we maintain our sense of unworthiness. The more we realize our unworthiness, the more we will value His love. No one will be grateful for that which he believes he has earned, deserves or is his by right. Therefore, the more legalist we become, the less grateful we will be. It is only because His love is bestowed freely, and contrary to merit, that it produces gratitude and thus love. "He that is forgiven much loves much."[488]

It is love that renders our service delightful to both God and us. When done simply as a mere legal duty, it is both as burdensome to us as it is offensive to God. Such service loses all value in the sight of God, because it has lost sight of the value of God. Our eyes always follow their true object of worship. It is only by eyeing God that all our acts of worship find acceptance with Him. If done while eyeing man's praise, they mock God by setting up man in His place as the real object of worship. The consumer-driven church, by eyeing the customer first, can never find acceptance with God, no matter how much it can point to the outer results for the justification of its actions before men. "For the Lord seeth not as man seeth; for man looketh on the outward appearance, but the Lord looketh on the heart."[489]

While it is true that the test of the reality of our worship of God is a life consecrated to the service of God alone, even the consecrated life must be tested. And the test of the reality of consecration is motives. This is the essence of the *Sermon on the Mount*, and the evidence of a new nature. For whose benefit are all my acts of service in His name, God's or mine? Or is my service related more to others (how moral, respectable or spiritual I look to them), rather than how glorious God appears to me? Such service, far from being consecration, is nothing but desecration. Consumerism seeks the knowledge of an affirming god; not one whose holiness demands our total allegiance, but one who champions our self-alliance and selfish aspirations.

The advancement of the Kingdom of God is synonymous with the advancement of the work of God in the soul. To eliminate this work of God in the soul is to invent a counterfeit Christianity that seeks to move

---

[488] Luke 6:47.
[489] 1 Samuel 16:7.

man to act by motivations that are consistent with his fallen nature. Christianity, then, becomes a mere business that can be manipulated by applying universal laws and principles that always render the desired results. But the extension of Christ's Kingdom cannot be measured by outward results alone. His Kingdom is concerned more with motives than actions. If those motives point to self, then the actions are in vain.[490] Listen as John Owen explains why it is vain to attempt to alter life's course without exchanging its Object by a spiritual and saving light,

> There is in this gospel holiness, as the spring and principle of it, a spiritual, saving light, enabling the mind and understanding to know God in Christ, and to discern spiritual things in a spiritual, saving manner; for herein God shines into our hearts, to give us the knowledge of His glory in the face of Jesus Christ, 2 Cor. iv. 6. Without this, in some degree, whatever pretense there may be or appearance of holiness in any, there is nothing in them of what is really so, and thereon accepted with God. Blind devotion, (that is, an inclination of mind unto religious duties, destitute of this light) will put men on a multiplication of duties, especially such as are of their own invention, in a show of wisdom in will-worship, and humility, and neglecting of the body, as the apostle speaks, Col. ii.23; wherein there is nothing of gospel holiness.[491]

It is all consumerism, unless our motive in all that we do is because we, having come to truly know Him, love Him with all our hearts, soul, mind and strength. The love that proceeds from the true knowledge of God renders a life of consecration unavoidable. And the only reason love does not proceed, is because idolatry remains. We know that we have been delivered from our idolatry when He, and no one, nor anything else, is the lover of our soul. In contrast to the spiritual weakness that accompanies

---

[490] Galatians 6:15, Romans 2:28,29.

[491] John Owen, *The Works of John Owen D.D.*, Vol. V (London and Edinburgh: Johnstone and Hunter; 1851), 433.

spiritual consumerism, Edwards describes the spiritual strength that accompanies those who love God for Himself,

> The same also appears from what has been observed of the nature of that spiritual knowledge, which is the foundation of all holy affections, as consisting in a sense and view of that excellency in divine things, which is supreme and transcendent. For hereby these things appear above all others, worthy to be chosen and adhered to. By the sight of the transcendent glory of Christ, true Christians see Him worthy to be followed; and so are powerfully drawn after Him; they see Him worthy that they should forsake all for Him: by the sight of that superlative amiableness, they are thoroughly disposed to be subject to Him, and engaged to labor with earnestness and activity in His service, and made willing to go through all difficulties for His sake. And it is the discovery of this excellency of Christ, that makes them constant to Him; for it makes a deep impression upon their minds, that they cannot forget Him; and they will follow Him whithersoever He goes, and it is in vain for any to endeavor to draw them away from Him.[492]

---

[492] Edwards, *Works*, Vol. III, 187.

PART III

DISCIPLESHIP:

The Life that Cherishes the Preeminence of Christ

"If a man hath a rich commodity, and one comes and offers half the worth of it, he takes it as a contempt; if it be not worth this, it is worth nothing. So the Lord is worthy of all our love, our lives, our souls, (though we had a thousand of them); and will a man not part with his lusts for Him? I tell you, the Lord takes Himself slighted, contemned, and loathed; if not worth all a man's love, He is worth nothing."[493]

Thomas Shepard

---

[493] Thomas Shepard, *The Parable of the Ten Virgins Opened and Applied* (Morgan: Soli Deo Gloria, 1997; original, 1695), 28.

CHAPTER 13

Called From A Self-Centered Life

From that time forth began Jesus to shew unto His disciples, how that He must go unto Jerusalem, and suffer many things of the elders and chief priest and scribes, and be killed, and be raised again the third day. Then Peter took Him, and began to rebuke Him, saying, Be it far from Thee, Lord: this shall not be unto Thee. But He turned, and said unto Peter, Get thee behind Me, Satan, thou art an offence unto Me: for thou savourest not the things that be of God, but those that be of men. Then said Jesus unto His disciples, If any man will come after Me, let him deny himself, and take up his cross, and follow Me. For whoever will save his life shall lose it: and whosoever will lose his life for My sake shall find it.

Mathew 16:21-25

Christ's call to follow is only the continuation of His original call to come. It is only with the full intention to follow that we can properly heed His call to come. But for those who are consumer-driven, it is far easier to simply call men to believe, without defining the implications of what it means to truly believe. Christ's call to come unto Him can never be separated from His call to come after Him. The fact that the latter call can never precede the former, does not invalidate the fact that it always proceeds from it. When Christ describes discipleship, He is only defining the implications of what it means to truly believe. All who reject the necessity of discipleship, reject the cost that is inherent in the very nature of a living faith. Faith must express itself, otherwise it is dead.[494] And if faith has Christ for its Object, then this expression will manifest in a life of conformity to that Object. "We cannot expect living fruit from a dead tree," says J. J. Oosterzee, "where, however, there is life," he continued, "it is not only desirable, but absolutely necessary, that the fruit be shown in a suitable form."[495]

Discipleship implies that the walk of faith is one that is characterized by self-denial rather than self-gratification. In no way does Christ insinuate that we are saved by our discipleship, but rather that the cause (our union with Him through faith) can never be without the effect (a life of following Him by faith in discipleship). While salvation is offered freely, we must never divide the cause from the effect by offering salvation freely, while making the effects of salvation optional. John Owen links the inseparable union that exist between both cause and effect in salvation when he wrote,

> It is true, our interest in God is not built upon our
> holiness; but it is as true that we have none without it.[496]

Thomas Robinson makes it clear that this inseparable union does not imply equal merit when he writes,

> The heavenly felicity is given to none but the holy; and
> yet it is not given on account of their holiness.[497]

Since we can never come to Christ without the full intention to follow Him, it is important, then, that we do not conceal the cost involved in following Him from those whom we exhort to come unto Him. To leave out discipleship when calling men to Christ is to leave Christ out of our

---

[494] James 2:26.

[495] J. J. Oosterzee, *Christian Dogmatics* (London: Hodder and Stoughton, 1874), 651.

[496] Owen, *Works*, Vol. XIII, 576.

[497] Thomas Robinson, *The Christian System Unfolded in a Course of Practical Essays on the Principle Doctrines and Duties of Christianity* (Glasgow: D. Mackenzie, 1830), 306.

call, or to call them to an ambiguous christ who is undeserving, because undefined. According to Dietrich Bonhoeffer,

> Christianity without discipleship is always Christianity without Christ."[498]

And this is the Christianity of preference today. John Duncan concurs with Bonhoeffer when he writes,

> the world likes a crowned Savior tolerably well, if it is a crown without a cross, but not a crucified Savior to draw men to be crucified![499]

The three prerequisites that Christ requires of those who would come after Him are: self-denial, cross-bearing, and finally following Him. The call to Christ is a call from a self-centered life. But before anyone can deny himself, he must first be able to clearly define what that self is that he must deny. Thomas Hooker characterized self-denial as "the Christian's first chief lesson." In his treaties, he defines self,

> when a man places a kind of supremacy or excellency in himself, or anything he doth or hath besides Christ; whereinsoever we place sufficiency or excellency besides in Christ, that is self.[500]

When man places the supremacy on his fleshly desires, that is self-indulgence. When he places a sufficiency on his own righteousness, that is self-righteousness. When man places the excellency on himself, that is idolatrous self-love.

Self-love is not defined as merely loving oneself but loving oneself above God. Therefore, self-love is hatred of God, or some part of God.

---

[498] Dietrich Bonhoeffer, *The Cost of Discipleship* (New York: Touch Stone, 1995: original, 1937), 59.

[499] John Duncan, *The Drawing Power of the Cross* (Grand Rapids: The Inheritance Publishers), 31.

[500] Thomas Hooker, *The Christian's Two Chief Lessons* (Ames: International Outreach Inc., 1997; original, 1640), 33.

Self hates God not as He is good, but as He dethrones self to set Himself up supreme. As long as self can continue to reign supreme, many would not object to Christ as Savior. But we can have no part with Him as Savior if we take up arms against Him as King. It is possible for carnal self-love to embrace Him as a Savior who saves, while rejecting Him as a King who rules. In both cases self maintains the supremacy. Furthermore, some would not abject to Christ as King so long as their submission to Him was meritorious, exalting the excellency of self, while rejecting the sufficiency of Christ' s work as the meritorious cause of salvation. "Hence the unbridled license of theoretical and practical Antinomianism," says J. J. Van Oosterzee, "is as immoral and antichristian as the self-righteousness of the Pharisaic Legalism."[501] Self finds expression in both and can equally reign in either.

Whenever self-love places either the supremacy or the sufficiency upon itself, defeat is inevitable. We cannot expect victory without the complete surrender of self, for real victory is not only over sin and Satan, but self as the foothold of Satan, and the root of sin in our lives, in all of its manifestations. Since both the dominion of Satan and sin are broken in the lives of the believer, self, too, is crucified, and should be reckoned dead and buried.[502]

Self-denial is nothing but the mortification of self, cross-bearing is the crucifixion of self, and following Christ is the forsaking of self. These are difficult, yea, impossible to those who are supremely in love with themselves. When men cry down the claims of Christ, it is because they love self. Those controlled by self-love will always find those commands difficult that cross self; whereas, those who submit to His yoke will find His burden light. Unless self be denied, the cross will not be properly taken up, nor Christ correctly followed.

Herein lies the problem. Since self-love favors a selfish gospel, we find it much easier to call men to receive the benefits of Christ without calling them to follow Him. We begin to market the gospel by changing it to appear more attractive to the lost. But the gospel, which is the power of God unto salvation, [503] loses its power to save once it is changed. The only

---

[501] Van Oosterzee, *Dogmatics*, 651.

[502] Romans 6:6 – 7; John 8:34 – 36.

[503] Romans 1:16.

way we can adorn the gospel, then, is not by changing it to conform more with the lives of those who are lost, but by conforming our lives more to it.[504] We cannot change it without diluting it. Nor can we make it more rationally appealing to the lost, for "the preaching of the cross is to them that perish foolishness."[505]

If we adorn the gospel with a faithful walk, then we can just as easily bring reproach upon it with an unfaithful walk, one that excludes discipleship. To the degree that the church conceals the cost of discipleship, it ignores its calling and undermine the effectiveness of its witness. The goal of those who first turned the world upside down was not pleasuring the consumer but following the Savior in paying the ultimate sacrifice. While it is solely the power of the gospel that saves, and not the power of our example, one of the greatest evidences of the truth of the gospel is the lives of those who were its eye witnesses. As their sacrifice bore witness to the reality of their message, so the message of a church driven to indulge the desires of the consumer bears false witness. Andrew Fuller said,

> We may justly consider our unchristian conduct as bearing false witness of God; for it is giving false representation of his gospel and government to the world. A grasping selfish spirit is saying to those around us, that, after all which we have professed of living by faith in a portion beyond death, the present world is the best, and therefore we are for making sure of that, and running all hazards as to the other.[506]

Implicit in the call to follow Christ is the call to forsake all other objects; "Follow me, and I will make you fishers of men. And they straightway left their nets, and followed Him."[507] "They forsook all, and followed Him."[508] Discipleship is non-negotiable. This is not a works-righteousness, for we only forsake that which competes with Christ and

---

[504] Titus 2:10.

[505] 1 Corinthians 1:18.

[506] Andrew Fuller, *The Backslider* (New York: The American Tract Society, 1840), 77.

[507] Matthew 4:19 – 20.

[508] Luke 5:11,28.

hinders us from following Him, self-righteousness being included among these hindrances. You cannot bribe nor lure one to the greater with the promise of the lesser. If all must be forsaken to follow Christ, then nothing could be offered but what would lure one away from Him. If we seek to sell Christ with lesser things, we make Him that much more inaccessible. You cannot barter One who is priceless. The very attempt to sell Him, is to devalue Him. As in the California gold rush, you do not have to convince one to pay the price to buy a field, once he has seen the treasure buried therein. The counterfeit offers of a consumer-driven church are successful only to lure those who value self above Christ. "It is not the willing," says Bernard, "but the unwilling that we woo with promises and rewards."[509]

The success of this glittering gospel does not only vindicate it in the eyes of much of the church, it also renders the real gospel a threat and a danger in their eyes. While it is true that the gospel of works is a deplorable heresy, since it puts one's dependency upon himself and his own ability, thus seeking to rob Christ of His glory, even more subtle is the gospel that does not call men to receive the whole Christ, and then to wholly follow the Christ received (not as the cause of salvation, but the goal of the salvation once received). Such a call denies both the sufficiency and excellency of Christ; His sufficiency to deliver from the power of sin, His excellency by making Him an agent of sin. This latter gospel is idolatrous, because its primary purpose is to spare the fallen nature of man, instead of exalting the excellencies of God; therefore, it denies both the need and the power of godliness in the lives of all who call upon Him.[510]

Although these man-centered gospels may produce the most results, they do not produce the right results. And even if the wrong gospel, through the sovereignty of God, produced the right results in some cases, the end does not justify the means. Therefore, it should never be endorsed by the church as a viable means to some good. Let us not deceive ourselves, using carnal means is the surest indication that we have carnal ends in view. Having carnal ends implies a state of enmity against God.[511] By looking too much to the benefits of man first, we lose sight of the real

---

[509] Bernard, *Bernard of Clairvaux: Selected Works* (Mahwah: Paulist Press, 1987), 188.
[510] 2 Timothy 2:19
[511] Romans 8:7.

end of the gospel, God's glory. We, by our sin, have all fallen short of that glory.[512] But for this reason we were both created and recreated, to reflect that glory. "This," according to Abraham Booth, "is the end for which Jehovah Himself acts, in all His works, both of providence and grace, so it is the highest end at which we can possibly aim."[513]

We must call men to God only in such a way that honors Him. The very gospel that we preach is designed to humble man as it exalts God. If it does not accomplish this, then it is not the gospel. God would despise His own nature if He redeemed us in such a way whereby self-loved continued to reign supreme in opposition to Him. It makes little difference whether this self-love reigns in self-righteousness or self-indulgence. Since the Spirit's application of redemption will never contradict God's intent in redemption (for the glory of His grace;[514] that we should be holy;[515] not of works lest anyone should boast[516]), then neither should our preaching contradict His intention. Gardinar Spring wrote,

> A selfish religion is an unreasonable religion, because it sets the less above the greater, and exalts the finite above the infinite; while a self-denying religion commends itself to reason and conscience, because it sets the greater above the less, and exalts the infinite above the finite.[517]

The gospel "is the power of God unto salvation for everyone who Believes."[518] Unless that gospel, once applied, excludes all boasting on the part of man, and makes one holy, it is either wrongly applied, not truly believed, or not true altogether. To believe in such a gospel is to accuse the omnipotent and omniscient God of lacking sufficient power and wisdom to conceive of no better way of redeeming sinful man than by allowing him to remain unrepentant and unchanged in his rebellion towards Him.

---

[512] Romans 3:23.

[513] Booth, *Reign of Grace*, 204.

[514] Ephesians 1:16,12.

[515] Ephesians 1:4, 5:25 – 27; Romans 8:29.

[516] Ephesians 2:9

[517] Gardinar Spring, *The Attraction of the Cross* (Carlisle: The Banner of Truth Trust, 1982; original, 1845), 191.

[518] Romans 1:16.

This would not only contradict His holiness, but His goodness which leads us to repentance[519] and turns us from our iniquities. "Sent Him to bless you, in turning away every one of you from his iniquities."[520] Such a gospel would not be a reason for rejoicing, as many make it, but the sad consequence of a god who was overpowered and outwitted by one more powerful and wiser than himself, and so forced into a relationship with man whereby he accommodates man's fallen nature by denying his own essential qualities, instead of implanting them.

We reprioritize the gospel, because we believe that the real one has become irrelevant or has lost its power. Realizing that man is depraved, we use the flesh to lure him into our midst. All of this is done under the veneer of morality, of course; otherwise, it would be easily detected as false, even by the world. The fact that man is by nature selfish does not give the church the right to manipulate his selfishness to its own advantage. The church, by offering primarily those things that are consistent with middle-class values, seeks to attract middle-class America unto itself, instead of Christ, who should be its biggest draw, and whose call to discipleship contradicts these very values.

Middle class values do not express the essence of discipleship. Most lost people do not want to raise disciples, but they do want to introduce their children into groups where they will have good role models and peers that might keep them away from the rampant use of drugs, sex, alcohol and violence among teens today, so long as discipleship is not the real goal. And the church is more than willing to offer all these things, and more, while stressing only the cultural morality (or lack thereof) that feeds the need for these programs to begin with, ignoring real discipleship altogether. There is nothing wrong with programs that are beneficial to society. The problem is that these things are not used in the church for growth in discipleship, but growth in numbers; not to call them to discipleship, but to comfort them in their non-discipleship. The whole mission of the church has been changed from that of making disciples, to merely catering to the needs of the non-disciples. The goal is not to reveal the awesomeness of God, but to show those who come into our midst that He is not such an awesome and fearful Being at all. And His demands are not as stringent as many

---

[519] Romans 2:4.
[520] Acts 3:26.

suppose. "In fact," we say, "He is really like you, and seeks the very same things that you seek – your own personal preferences."

This is not the example we find in Christ. He lets us know right from the start that our relationship with Him is not one where we are expecting Him to perform up to the expectations of our self-love, but one which involves self-denial, whereby we are expected to love Him above ourselves.[521] Richard Chenevix Trench reiterated this truth when he wrote,

> The great Captain of our salvation, never keeps back or conceals what those who faithfully witness for Him may have to bear for His name's sake; never entices recruits into His service, or seeks to retain them under His banner, by promises that they shall find all things easy and pleasant there. So far from this, He says of Paul at the outset of his apostolic career, 'I will show him how great things he must suffer for My name's sake' (Acts 9:16).[522]

When we describe the Christian life as something other than following Christ, or attempt to enhance the gospel with things other than Christ, we are only calling men away from Christ.

We are unchristlike, then, whenever we ignore self-denial, refuse to call men from a self-centered life, or seek to customize our church activities and messages to the desire of man, rather than the glory of God. This is not the example of the One who spoke nothing of Himself, but only what the Father gave Him.[523] Rather, this is the example of those who "loved the praise of men more than the praise of God."[524] If man desires shorter, less frequent services, we will cater to their desires in order to keep those in the church who would otherwise leave and attend elsewhere. But some may ask, "Why would any non-disciple even attend church at all?" When the church is set on exalting human selfishness above the glory of God, the

---

[521] Matthew 10:16 – 31; Luke 9:23; John 16:2 – 33; Ezekiel 2:3 – 7; Jeremiah 1:19.

[522] Richard Chenevix Trench, *The Seven Churches in Asia* (London: MacMillan and CO., 1867), 105.

[523] John 13:49.

[524] John 12:43.

price of attending church becomes far less than the price of not attending at all. Men seek respectability and a clear conscience at the lowest price possible. And, like a retail chain, the consumer-driven church is more than willing to lower its price below that of all its competitors. To be sure, there is a legalistic name-brand church that also appeals to the flesh, for there are always those who will overpay to win the title of best dressed, but, as it stands today, the crowds are flocking to the discount outlets where the price to wear the name Christian is drastically reduced.

Discipleship, the anti-consumer disposition, is no longer stressed, because it would certainly reduce their numbers, just as it reduced the number of followers when Christ stressed the cost of discipleship. Instead, we only stress the benefits, and even add a few of our own. We promise health, wealth, peace, comfort, self-esteem and promote self-help, because these are the primary messages of self-love. If the preaching of the cross is foolishness, then the preaching of self will be considered wisdom. What we try to reconcile is not their hearts with Christ, but Christ with their consumer lifestyle. And all who cherish the counterfeit offers of a consumer culture, will be drawn to this counterfeit christ.

Christ said, "And I, if I be lifted up from the earth, will draw all men unto Myself."[525] One would have to wonder, does the church resort to such measures because Christ has lost his drawing power, or has Christ ceased to draw because He is no longer lifted up? Christ is no longer exalted when we preach Christ the man pleaser, rather than "Christ crucified, unto the Jews' a stumbling-block, and unto the Greeks foolishness."[526] Any gospel that gives the preeminence to man is an attack on the preeminence of Christ. We deny the power of the gospel when we think that our finite powers and selfish appeals are necessary to draw men.

The church becomes consumer-driven whenever it "savourest not the things that be of God, but the things that be of men." Such a church would not abject to having money changers and those who buy and sell in the temple, so long as the church is benefited and the outward participation in worship is made less demanding. It is certainly a satanic influence that instigate the present-day call, which appeals primarily to the things of

---

[525] John 12:32.
[526] 1 Corinthians 1:23.

men. What was Christ's response to such an appeal from Peter that focused primarily on comforting man:

> Get thee behind Me, Satan: for thou savourest not the things that be of God, but the things that be of men.[527]

Satan's accusation of Job was really an attack on God Himself. "Put forth Thine hand now and touch all that he hath, and he will curse Thee to Thy Face."[528] Job's response was proof that his motive in serving God was not one of self-interest. It was God and not His gifts that he sought. "The Lord gave, and the Lord hath taken away; Blessed be the name of the Lord."[529] Satan's accusation, while false in the case of Job, is true of many today. Take away all benefits and you take away all religion. Satan accusation implies that unless God paid the sinner to serve Him, no one would serve God at all; that God, in and of Himself, is not sufficiently attractive to draw anyone to Himself. And those who do seemingly join themselves to Him, would quickly forsake Him without these added benefits.

When we insert things in the gospel to entice men to serve God, or leave those things out that are essentially vital to it, we affirm the veracity of Satan's accusations. When we preach a gospel catered to the interest of the lost, we imply that there is not enough in Christ to compel men to come. The only difference is that Satan believed that Job would forsake God under the most strenuous affliction, while we are fearful that the modern Christian would forsake Him for the least offence or slightest inconvenience. Therefore, consumer-driven Christianity is a modern repeat of the proclamation of Satan – that there is no such thing as disinterested devotion to God; that there is no real devotion at all in the world. It is a proclamation that the gift is more valuable than the Giver. It affirms that no one will love God for Himself, and that He is not the exceeding and great reward of His people. It is a denial, if not of the existence, then certainly of the nature, excellency and power of God. It is a denial of both the sufficiency of God alone to fully satisfy the soul

---

[527] Mark 8:33.
[528] Job 1:11.
[529] Job 1:21.

of man and of man's greatest responsibility to make God his chief end. It is, then, a satanic attack on the church.

True discipleship is impossible whenever we lower the requirements or exaggerate the benefits in order to persuade men to join our church. The first implies that they will reject the requirements, thereby insisting on their own preeminence. The second implies that they will despise so great a salvation unless we offer them some extra benefits that go along with it. But it is precisely from this consumer way of thinking that Christ calls us. The true convert chooses Christ as his portion. And the test of the one who so chooses Christ, is that he cannot be content, offer him whatever you may, with anything less than Christ. "There can be no genuine religion," said Gardinar Spring, "where God is not the chief joy."[530] One will certainly enjoy many things that accompany salvation and are provided in connection with the church, but he cannot be content with any of these things apart from Christ, his greatest treasure. It is to Him that all the ordinances, spiritual disciplines and church activities point.

We cannot call men to the greatest Object while disproportionately pointing to all the lesser objects that men hope to gain by Him. If we were convinced of the greatness of Christ, we would see no need to lure men to Him by pointing to all those other things. Any such attempt would deny the greatness of Christ in the mind of those who hear us and make Him the means to some end that they deem superior; a servant rather than a Lord. "You seek Me, not because you saw the signs, but because you ate of the loaves and were filled."[531] While it is true that Christ "went about doing good, and healing all that were oppressed of the devil,"[532] He would not have the good that He does be the main reason why people respond to Him. According to David Clarkson,

> The end gives nature and name to the action. If your
> aims be legal, mercenary, the act will be so. Go not about

---

[530] Gardinar Spring, *Fragments from the Study of a Pastor,* Vol. I (New York: John S. Taylor, 1838), 138.

[531] John 6:26.

[532] Acts 10:38.

it only to escape hell, avoid wrath, satisfy justice, pacify conscience.[533]

One thing is certain, you cannot call men to the greatest Object by luring them with lesser objects, because the same object with which you lure them, is also the object to which you lure them.

While we must never ignore, but fully trust in all the promises of God (since these reveal His character, which is the real object of trust), we must also realize that the church will fail in their great commission to go and make disciples of all nations, to the extent that it fails to fully present the work, claims, and character of Christ to the nations. To the degree that they present partial notions of Christ, they fail in their greatest purpose, and only gather disciples after themselves. If the preaching of Christ crucified is sufficient to draw the elect, then those whose preaching is characterized by enticing words of human wisdom, seek to attract a larger audience than that which they believe the gospel alone could reach. S. M. Woodbridge warns,

> Religion is made easy only by debasing its quality. While human nature is what it is, there can be no way of exalting human power in the affair of conversion to God, except by degrading religion itself into conformity to the tastes of the unrenewed heart.[534]

We cannot call men to Christ in any other way than that by which He called men to Himself. The way to call them from a self-centered life is not by appealing to their selfishness. Nor can we offer anything less than what Christ offers to men. The first thing that Christ offers is a cross. By doing so, He does not seek to make it as easy as possible for as many as possible to come to Him. I know this thought is near blasphemy to the consumer-driven church, and immediately brings accusations of injustice, but to do anything less than to clearly define the terms of discipleship to the lost, is to do them the injustice of deceiving them with a non-cross-bearing

---

[533] David Clarkson, *The Practical Works of David Clarkson*, Vol. I (Edinburgh: James Nichol, 1864), 19.

[534] S. M. Woodbridge, from *The Princeton Review*, Vol. 14 No. 1, 1842, 12.

message of comfort and ease that is inspired by none other than Satan himself.[535] God has given men the right to reject His call, but we deprive them of this right by giving them only such an offer that we know they will not refuse. Our preaching has not failed every time someone rejects it, but may merely have been correctly stated.

---

[535] Matthew 16:23

CHAPTER 14

The Cost of Discipleship

If any man come to Me, and hate not his father, and mother, and wife, and children, and brethren, and sisters, yea, and his own life also, he cannot be My disciple. And whosoever doth not bear his cross, and come after Me, cannot be My disciple. For which of you, intending to build a tower, sitteth not down first, and counteth the cost, whether he have sufficient to finish it? Lest haply, after he hath laid the foundation, and is not able to finish it, all that behold it begin to mock him, saying, This man began to build, and was not able to finish. Or what king, going to make war against another king, sitteth not down first, and consulteth whether he be able with ten thousand to meet him that cometh against him with twenty thousand? Or else, while the other is yet a great way off, he sendeth an ambassage, and desireth conditions of peace. So likewise, whosoever he be of you that forsaketh not all that he hath, he cannot be My disciple.

Luke 14:26-33

There are only two options. Those who do not receive Christ in the fullness of His character, offices, work and words, reject Him. "He that rejecteth Me, and receiveth not My words."[536] If we are to receive Him, however, we must do so on the terms clearly outlined in His teaching; otherwise, we reject Him. Martyn Lloyd-Jones wrote,

> Having the Kingdom of God in your heart means that
> you accept His teaching.[537]

Those who refuse any of Christ's terms, or proclaim they are of another dispensation, are excluded from His Kingdom. No one is permitted to change His words or lower His claim over our lives to suit one's own preferences. For the moment we reserve the right to refuse any of the principles of His Kingdom expressed in His teaching, we reject His right to make any claim whatsoever over our lives. To reject any of His terms is to reject His person, and thus His offer on our behalf. Therefore, whether we are a disciple-making church or not, depends more on how we define discipleship and follow His teachings, than on our ability to implement activities and programs, whether within or outside of the church, that increase membership involvement. Since discipleship is primarily a heart issue, our ability to rally the troops to any given cause is least likely to influence the true disciple whose loyalty to Christ cannot be divided, and who now views the whole of his life as one continual witness for Christ.

When we focus primarily on the outward mission, we are inviting the flesh to show us its power and zeal. And the more radical we become, the more we entice men to make a great show in the flesh.[538] The more we focus on Christ and Christlikeness, however, the more we will promote spiritual sacrifices acceptable to God through Christ. The difference between the two is a new creation or a Pharisee; sincerity or a mere show. The former has no ulterior motives, but seeks to be transparent as he faithfully exalts the glory of God in both heart and life. The latter seeks to control others with methods and techniques that manipulate the flesh, all under the guise of piety. But it is not until the great commission becomes an expression of the great commandment that the fruit that ensues will be genuine

---

[536] John 12:47 – 48.
[537] Martyn Lloyd-Jones, *The Kingdom of God* (Wheaton: Credo Publishing Corperation, 1992), 64.
[538] 2 Corinthians 11.

discipleship, rather than a superficial Christianity that indiscriminately swallows every counterfeit that man can devise.[539]

We should not praise ourselves for accepting some of His terms, for partial submission is rebellion. Even the unregenerate would crown Christ as king over their lives on their own terms.[540] But unlike the consumer-driven church, Christ would not reign over any multitude upon false pretenses. He must reveal Himself for who He is, thereby always ruining the true intentions of the multitude. Nor does He reign in any heart that conflicts with His mission or person. Unless we receive Him as the Bible sets Him forth, we only reject Him, thereby failing to find His eternal qualities so compelling that we fervently and completely forsake all to follow Him. Those who reject the terms of discipleship, therefore, reveal that they are not His disciples. Thomas Boston shows the mind-set of those who are in a true covenant relationship with God, when he wrote,

> They are such as cordially approve of and acquiesce in
> the plan of the covenant, as suited to the honour of God,
> and to their particularly looking upon it as well ordered
> in all things (2 Sam 23:5).[541]

We hesitate to fully receive Him for who He is, because we do not find who He is supremely desirable. Our hesitation reveals that there is something in our life that competes with Him for supreme affection. This we fear to lose and will not give up.

The consumer-driven church, by nature, will always strive to conform the Word into the mold of its consumer's interest. Such a church, in order to validate its own existence and extend its influence, will always attempt to justify whatever interest the customer may have that could be utilized to attract him to the church. How we do church, then, depends on the preferences of the customer. If the customer does not find God desirable, then He must be changed. Hence, contrary to the aims of the

---

[539] Ephesians 4:14.
[540] John 6:15, 26, 27.
[541] Thomas Boston, *A View of the Covenant of Grace from the Sacred Records,* (Glasgow: R Chapman, 1707), 229.

true ministers of God,[542] many take it upon themselves to make Him more desirable by removing those aspects of His Word and nature that are in conflict with a consumer culture. Abraham Kuyper describes the process,

> They who in other respects are faithful Christians have abandoned far too greatly the personal elements in the living God, and in turn dote on the beautiful ideas of mercy and love, of peace and the higher good.....the trouble is that instead of saying, 'God is love' or 'love is God,' one forms an idea of love which eclipses God from sight. And estranged from the living God, one dotes on creations of his own thought.[543]

Once He is redefined into the mold of our consumer interests, discipleship becomes only a reaffirmation of self.[544] Any concept of following Christ that does not include supreme love, will inevitably be a mere following of self.

Nominal Christianity is the result of attaching ourselves to Christianity for ourselves with no change of heart or attachment to Christ. It makes Christianity a consumer enterprise that competes with other entities for the attention of the consumer by appealing to his desires. This is why the consumer appeal excludes discipleship. None can argue that he desires Christ but finds His terms too difficult to receive. His terms only flow from His person. We think His terms are too demanding, only because we

---

[542] 1 Thessalonians 2:3 – 6.

[543] Abraham Kuyper, *To Be Near unto God* (Grand Rapids: Eerdmans-Sevensma Co., 1918), 65.

[544] "Natural men may indeed shape a covenant, in their own apprehensions, into such a form, as they may have a very good liking of it. They may apprehend it as a covenant designed to make men easy and happy; while in the meantime it allows them, at least in some instances to be unholy; as a covenant wherein, though Christ's means, they may obtain acceptance with God by their good works, notwithstanding of their ill works. But in all this they are in love with a creature of their own fancy, not with God's covenant of grace. Let the covenant be set before them in the light of Scriptures, and viewed in that light; they will be sure to dislike it, and pick holes in it." Boston, *A View of the Covenant of Grace*, 230.

think too much of ourselves and too little of Him. If real love for Christ exists in the heart, then His claims become our delight. They are only burdensome to those who are contrary to them. Even the unregenerate will gladly receive a Christ that reflects their own values. But, much like the Jews who cried out at one time, "hosanna,"[545] the moment Christ fails to meet our expectations, we immediately cry out, "crucify Him."[546]

The important thing is not that we desire Christ, but from whence do these desires proceed. Love for oneself, or Christ? If such desires proceed from a love for self, we will not be humbled by our contrariness to Him, but pridefully try to reinvent Him according to our own desires. All love for this transformed Christ is only love for our own desires. Ralf Erskine explains why this is always the case,

> Walking in Christ," he says, "excludes a walking in self;
> for the more that a man walks in Christ, the more does
> he walk out of self; as Christ comes in self goes out; when
> Christ is received self is expelled.[547]

If His claim over our life becomes a burden or a disappointment, then we have not taken them up with any thought of Christ, but only with the thought of what self might gain from Him. It is self that becomes burdened and disappointed with Christ whenever we are commanded to do that which self does not desire, or fails to receive that which self expected. Disobedience becomes the greatest burden to those who really love Christ and want to do His will. Complying with His terms becomes their greatest delight. Does this imply that there is no cost in discipleship for those who find it their delight? On the contrary, for the more one delights in Christ, the greater the battle one will have with the flesh, which is contrary to Him. Christ only reigns in the heart that is in conflict with His enemies. Therefore, consumer-driven Christianity, by diminishing the seriousness of this conflict, proves itself a counterfeit. Bishop John Charles Ryle describes this counterfeit Christianity:

---

545 Matthew 21:9.

546 Matthew 27:23.

547 Ralf Erskine, *The Sermons and Other Practical Writings of the Revered and Learned Ralf Erskine,* Vol. III (London: R. Baynes, 1821), 52.

I grant freely that it cost little to be a mere outward Christian. A man has only got to attend a place of worship twice on Sunday, and to be tolerably moral during the week, and he has gone as far as thousands around him ever go in religion. All this is cheap and easy work; it entails no self-denial or self-sacrifice. If this is saving Christianity, and will take us to heaven when we die, we must alter the description of the way of life, and write, wide is the gate and broad is the way that leads to heaven!.....A religion that costs nothing is worth nothing! A cheap Christianity, without a cross, will prove in the end a useless Christianity, without a crown.[548]

The genuine disciple of Christ gives Him an exclusive loyalty.[549] He puts the claims of Christ first, no matter the cost. Therefore, he is no real disciple who either subordinates Christ's claims to his own personal interests and plans, or who only follows Christ insofar as it accords with his own best interest and promotes his own plans. This statement does not undermine grace and gratitude, but rather underlines them. Would it not be the greatest ingratitude imaginable for the one who has experienced the incalculable riches of God's grace and understands the infinite price that was paid on his behalf to secure it, and his own utter unworthiness to receive it, to willfully hold back any part of his life from the lordship of Christ. Such a one would rather surrender all his being in the service of his Benefactor. And this he would do not only because God requires it, but because he sees that God is worthy of all. To purposely hold back part would be to hold back all.

To this end Christ died, that he might acquire this absolute lordship, especially in the life of the redeemed. "For to this end Christ died and rose and lived again that He might be Lord of both the dead and the living."[550] "Him God has exalted to His right hand to be Prince and Savior, to give

---

[548] J C Ryle, *Holiness* (London: James Clark and Co., 1956; reprint), 69,72.

[549] Mark 8:34 – 38; Luke 14:26 – 37.

[550] Romans 14:9.

repentance to Israel and forgiveness of sins."[551] If we desire that He be exalted in our lives, it will only be by desiring Him for all that He was exalted to be (a Prince as well as a Savior), and by receiving from Him all that he was exalted to give (repentance as well as forgiveness).

If Christ is our pattern, then the cross will be central in our message as well as our method. None can follow Christ unless he follows His example of self-denial and cross-bearing. We correctly comprehend Christ only when we perceive those qualities which He manifested in His life. We follow Him only so far as we take these qualities into our own lives. The main quality we see in the life of Christ is that he must, out of divine necessity, die to His own will, comfort, worldly honor, and even to those who are closest to Him, so that He may live for the will of the One who sent Him.

> Jesus began to show to His disciples that He <u>must</u> go to Jerusalem, and suffer many things from the elders and chief priests and scribes, and be killed, and be raised the third day.[552]

We deceive ourselves when we believe that we can follow Christ down any road other than the one which He has trodden. Even more, we deceive others when we declare to them some other way than the path of self-sacrifice and self-denial that Christ manifested on the cross. Self-denial implies that we cannot change Christ nor Christianity to conform to our desires but must accept Him as He is. Any change would imply self-indulgence.

Neither are we allowed to change Him to appear less offensive to the loss. If it is wrong to change Christ to suit one's own desires, then it is equally wrong to preach Him in such a way that suits the desires of the lost. Just as we can accept Him only as He is, so we must proclaim Him only as He is. While Christ is offered freely in the gospel, that gospel is not embraced until the freely offered Christ is embraced by faith. We can call men to no greater blessedness than that of conformity to the same spirit which Christ displayed in the sacrifice of Himself upon the cross. This

---

[551] Acts 5:31.
[552] Matthew 16:21.

means that those who call men to the most popular, easy and comfortable way, rob them of this blessedness by inviting them to enter by the wide gate that leads to destruction.

Dietrich Bonhoeffer expresses the essence of the true call of Christ when he writes,

When Christ calls a man, He bids him come and die.[553]

And A W Tozer describes the essence of cross-bearing when he writes,

> The cross is a symbol of death. It stands for the abrupt, violent end of a human being. In Romans times the man who took up this cross and started down the road was not coming back. He was not going out to have his life redirected. He was going out to have it ended! The cross did not try to keep on good terms with its victims. It struck cruel and hard, and when it had finished its work the man was no more![554]

We may not be called to take up a literal cross, but if we profess to be His disciples, we must possess that same love for Christ that would lead us to it, if the opportunity presented itself.[555] We must be ready to literally die for the cause of Christ. This readiness to die must presently manifest itself in a willingness to live for the glory of Christ as we die to our personal comfort, wealth, friends and honor for the cause of Christ. Far from seeking the easy life, it is a readiness to encounter mockery, cruelty, shame and suffering, as we pursue the path of discipleship for the glory of Christ; otherwise, we are not worthy to be called His disciples, and basically live for ourselves.

The great guilt of those who belittle discipleship, by declaring it

---

[553] Dietrich Bonhoeffer, *The Cost of Discipleship* (New York: Touch Stone, 1995: original, 1937), 11

[554] A W Tozer, *The Best of A.W. Tozer* (Grand Rapids: Baker Book House, 1978), 176.

[555] Matthew 10:38 – 39.

either optional or of secondary importance, is that they belittle Christ by placing the preferences of the consumer above, or even to the exclusion of, God's due. That worship that does not include presenting our bodies a living sacrifice is not only unreasonable, but unacceptable. Such a call does not only hinder men from pursuing their greatest duty, it also hinders them from pursuing their greatest privilege and encourages them in their greatest sin. He promotes the sin of all sins; the very sin of Satan himself – the sin of seeking to become his own god by declaring along with Pharoah, "who is the Lord, that I should obey His voice."[556]

Four Concluding Cautions
Caution #1

Although the essence of discipleship remains the same in all God's children, its degrees may vary according to the faith and growth of each child of God. Comparison in any area is never wise.[557] Greater humility is always a sign of greater growth.

Caution #2

It is not an act of discipleship, nor an act of non-discipleship that proves we are disciples or not, but the direction of the whole life as it proceeds from the heart toward God.

Caution #3

As God's covenant was ratified with the children of Israel before the giving of the Law (And all the people answered together, and said, "All that the Lord hath spoken we will do." And Moses returned the words of the people unto God),[558] so discipleship is entered into

---

[556] Exodus 5:2.
[557] 2 Corinthians 10:12.
[558] Exodus 19:8.

not after we understand all that God requires of us, but always with a willingness and full intention to obey all that we do know, or will come to know, without question. Disciples are ever learning and ever growing.[559]

Caution #4

Discipleship is not to be placed in our justification and regeneration, but in our conversion (turning to Christ) and sanctification (following Christ). We must always remember that the righteousness wherein we are justified is perfect, but not inherent; whereas, that wherein we are sanctified is inherent, but not perfect.

---

[559] 2 Peter 3:18.

CHAPTER 15

Faith, A Life-Changing Act

For as the body without the spirit is dead, so faith
without works is dead also.

James 2:26

I f we are to travel the pathway of discipleship, we must first become
disciples. Discipleship begins at conversion. While we are called to make
disciples, the first step in discipleship is conversion. The primary reason
that the church fails in its mission to make disciples is not an insufficient
stress on discipleship, but their lack of a thorough understanding of
what constitutes a genuine conversion. Any church, then, claiming to be
"missional", while failing to stress the need for a genuine conversion of
the heart, has a self-defeating mission. Experimental Christianity more
properly deserves the title missional. True religion must extend inward
before it can extend outward.[560]

Discipleship, like true faith, must be considered nonexistent without
works. But simply performing the outer acts of a disciple, according to the
Sermon on the Mount, does not make one a follower of Christ. Those who
radicalize the outer acts alone, do not promote discipleship. For the true
followers of Christ do not sound a trumpet before all their good works,
nor use them as an occasion to pat each other on the back. The Missional
church could easily become the new legalism, unless the inner life of the
heart be equally articulated. Experimental Christianity, that is of the

---

[560] James 1:27.

heart, ends in good works, but always begins with faith; "the life which I now live in the flesh I live by the faith of the Son of God."[561] It is the acts that spring from faith, in union with Christ, that show a changed heart.

The term disciple appears 274 times in the New Testament, while the term Christian only occurs 3 times. It was at Antioch that the disciples were first called Christians.[562] If we call ourselves Christians, it is only because we have first become His disciples. We become Christ's disciples by responding to His call in the proclamation of the Gospel. This call becomes effectual only when we respond with faith and repentance, both of which are the only proper response upon hearing the Gospel. "Repent therefore and be converted, that your sins may be blotted out."[563]

Repentance is the hand releasing the defiled object, while faith is the hand receiving the divine Object. These are not the meritorious cause of salvation (that being the blood of Christ alone), nor are they the efficient cause (that being the Spirit who applies salvation and Christ who is the author of life). But faith and repentance are the instrumental cause through which salvation is received. We are saved when we believe and repent, not because we believe and repent. Far from being meritorious, they are self-emptying.

Conversion is a going out of self, unto God. Faith and repentance are the first steps both out of and away from self, and into and towards God. Unless these steps be thoroughly taken, there can be no further approach unto God. Nor are these a onetime act, but the continuous habit of the soul. The only evidence of faith and repentance in the past are their continuation in the present. This is why Thomas Shepard exhorted believers to "be always converting and always converted."[564] John Duncan also challenges those who are resting in past experiences when he writes,

> All who have been drawn are being drawn still; and all who are being drawn are coming to Christ. They have heard Him who says 'Come!' and they have set out to go

[561] Galatians 2:20.

[562] Acts 11:26.

[563] Acts 3:19.

[564] Thomas Shepard, *The Works of Thomas Shepard*, Vol. II (Boston: Doctrinal Tract Society, 1835), 632.

to Him; He is always saying 'Come, come!' and they're coming and getting nearer. What steps of progress are we making as the result of this drawing? Surely, if we are not coming, He is not drawing.[565]

Referring particularly to the doctrine of repentance, many have insisted on the continual aspect of its nature:

"Repentance itself, instead of being a passing act, is an abiding principle, a lasting disposition of the soul, a gracious principle lying deep in the heart, disposing a man at all times to mourn for and turn from sin.... If, therefore, a man regards repentance only as the first stage in the way to heaven, and instead of renewing daily his exercise of it, satisfies himself with concluding that he has passed the first stage, the truth of his repentance is very questionable."[566]

John Colquhoun

"Repentance is not true and sound when it does not turn a man from all known sin to all known good, or when it does not continue in strength and actually renew itself continually from the time of conversion to the end of life."[567]

William Ames

"It is part of regeneration, an infused grace: therefore it does not vanish after its first act; that is contrary to the promise; nor does it continue idle, unexercised in the habit, till death; for that is contrary to the nature of grace; it is active, fruitful – active, when there is

---

[565] John Duncan, *The Drawing Power of the Cross* (Grand Rapids: The Inheritance Publishers), 29-30.

[566] John Colquhoun, *Repentance* (London: Banner of Truth Trust, 1965; original 1826), 26.

[567] William Ames, *The Marrow of Theology* (Grand Rapids: Baker Books, 1997; original, 1623), 160.

occasion. Sin, when committed, is an occasion to exercise repentance, or else there can be no occasion for it. Can an instance be given of any other grace whose exercise is never required, but immediately after its first infusion?"[568]

David Clarkson

"In sanctification, faith and repentance are not resolved, but continued and completed."[569]

J. J. Van Oosterzee

Spiritual illumination and the new birth are passively received, both being fully the work of God who gives sight to the blind and raises the dead. But that which is passively received cannot be passively possessed. Therefore, they always spring forth into faith and repentance, which are both gifts that are actively received, requiring man's full cooperation in the conversion of the soul. While regeneration is a spiritual change carried out by God, conversion is a spiritual motion carried out by man in faith and repentance. Faith and repentance are both the free gifts of God, as well as the soul's first response toward God. The same faith which is the gift of God, becomes an act in the believer the moment received. All faith that does not express itself in actions must be dead, or non-existent.[570]

While the acts of faith are indeed our actions, they are not of our creation. "Repenting and believing are properly man's acts," says Samuel Shaw, "and yet they are performed by God's power."[571] Therefore, they should not excite pride. Those who consider God as the source of these gifts will give glory to the giver of the gifts; not only by recognizing them as gifts, but also by employing them as such. Where the gift is valuable, ingratitude is impossible. And true gratitude, as well as true faith, renders

---

[568] David Clarkson, *The Practical Works of David Clarkson*, Vol. I (Edinburgh: James Nichol, 1864), 33.

[569] Van Oosterzee, *Christian Dogmatics*, 657.

[570] James 2:17.

[571] Samuel Shaw, *The Works of Rev. Samuel Shaw, M. A.* Vol. 1 (Boston: George Clark, 1821), 244.

boasting impossible.[572] While they are our doing, the moment we think they are of our doing, they quickly become our undoing.

The acts of faith and repentance do not give us some special claim on God, thereby obligating Him to act on our behalf in the salvation of our souls. They are an acknowledgement by us that we have no claim on God at all. Nor are they the evidence that we are somehow better than the rest of lost humanity for having performed them. These acts are our acknowledgement that we, as part of lost humanity, are helpless and in need of a Savior. Our real esteem for these gifts rises to the level of our gratitude (which reflects on Christ), and falls to the level of our boasting (which points to us). The moment we are proud of our discipleship, we have lost it. The moment we reckon the gift of God our own doing, we have no gratitude.

Today, far from esteeming repentance as a precious gift, many despise it by regarding it as optional, unimportant, or even dangerous to the doctrine of salvation by grace alone, erroneously considering it the work of man alone.[573] Such an attitude proves that one has never experienced it in his own heart. Or, if he has experienced it, he is certainly very ungrateful for it, and fails to see its absolute necessary to a life of holiness, which George Burder describes as a precious part of that salvation obtained by Christ,

> We are to esteem it a precious part of his salvation to be
> delivered from the slavery of the devil, and the tyranny
> of our native corruption. The doctrine of salvation,
> by grace, through faith, is so far from being contrary
> to holiness, or hurtful in good works, that it is God's
> powerful instrument of producing them.[574]

If we really considered this as a precious gift, we would desire it and encourage others to seek the same. But we do not encourage this, either

---

[572] Ephesians 2:8,9.

[573] This was not the sentiment of the early church; Acts 2:38, 3:19, 17:30, 20:21, 26:20.

[574] George Burder, *Village Sermons*, Vol. II (Philadelphia: W. W. Woodward, 1817), 20-21.

because we do not want to offend any potential customer, or because we do not count it as a gift worth encouraging nor receiving. Therefore, we could not have graciously received that which we refuse to publicly and enthusiastically endorse, but rather warn against as something of another dispensation.[575] Either our hearts are favorably inclined towards repentance, or they are disinclined towards it; therefore we either encourage it, or seek to rationally excuse it from our doctrine and life.

Faith, we say, is the gift that we should proclaim before men. But to despise either of the gifts of faith or repentance is to despise their source. Indifference or coldness towards either, proves a lack of the other. To redefine one is to eliminate the other. They both rise or fall together. The closer we draw near to God in faith, the further we will move from sin in repentance; the higher the faith, the deeper the repentance.

Faith and repentance are not two acts in conversion, they are two aspects of the very same act. If self and Christ are opposite, we cannot turn to one without turning from the other in the very same act. The work of grace cannot be divided. If we exalt faith while neglecting repentance, according to Charles Haddon Spurgeon, we really have no interest in faith at all. "To divide the work of grace," he says, "would be to cut the living child in halves, and those who would permit this have no interest in it."[576] Alexander Maclaren also describes their inseparableness when he writes,

> we can wrangle and squabble, as divided sects have done, about which comes first, the fact being, that though you can part them in thought, you cannot part them in experience, inasmuch as they are but the obverse and the reverse, the two sides of the same coin. Faith and repentance….they are done in one and the same indissoluble act.[577]

Repentance, like its sister grace of faith, also works by love. "What

---

[575] 2 Timothy 2:25, Ephesians 2:8.

[576] C H Spurgeon, *All of Grace* (Fort Worth: RDML Publishing, 2001; original 1880), 73.

[577] Alexander Maclaren, *Sermons Preached in Manchester* (London: Macmillan and Co., 1871), 173.

distinguishes penitence from remorse and from every other substitute is
the presence of love as the motive for shame and hatred of one's sins,"[578]
says Bishop Hall. That faith which does not manifest a turning from sin
in repentance, neither works by love for God.[579] We cannot but mourn for
those sins committed against a God we love, and we will not mourn, nor
forsake, those sins committed against a God toward whom our affections
are cold; unless some other love constrains us. G. S. Faber describes these
constraints when he writes,

> It is not sin that they hate, but the wages of sin, it is not
> God that they love, but their own safety.[580]

Thus, repentance, whether true or false, is impossible without love,
whether for ourselves or God, respectively. Many condemned criminals
have mourned for crimes committed, not for the wickedness of the crime,
but for the punishment pronounced upon them for the crime. Likewise,
many a false convert will have remorse for their sins, but this, while
included in real repentance, is not repentance. Like Judas, false repentance
may consist not only of much sorrow, but even of confession of sin. Such
repentance even caused Judas to throw down as worthless that same money
that prompted him to betray Christ to begin with. Thomas Scott reveals
how it is possible for the unregenerate to produce all these effects, and yet
remain unregenerate,

> If a man be ever so much terrified at the prospect of
> punishment, or ever so sorry for his conduct merely
> because it exposes him to suffering, there is nothing
> of repentance in it; even though he exclaims ever so
> vehemently against his own conduct, and make ever
> so many confessions, or even so much restitution or
> appear ever so much reformed or cry ever so earnestly

---

[578] Rev. Francis J Hall, *Introduction to Dogmatic Theology* (New York: Longmans, Green, and Co., 1907), 241.

[579] See chapter Fiftteen on *Love's Abhorrence*.

[580] G. S. Faber, *A Practical treatise on the Ordinary Operations of the Holy Spirit* (New York: Eastburn, Kirk and Co, 1814), 79.

for mercy. These things may consist with an unhumbled impenitent heart; and spring from self-love.[581]

Those who love holiness and hate evil must love repentance which forsakes the one and turns to the other. Many a false convert will turn from sins, not because he hates them, but only for the negative consequences that these sins pose to self; self-preservation constrains him. Many a false convert will turn to God, not out of love for Him, but because he seeks the benefits that come from Him; self-advantage constrains him. Self-preservation and self-advantage are not sinful in themselves; they only become so as the primary constraining force against evil and for good in our lives. While the true penitent can truthfully announce along with Paul "for the love of Christ constraineth us,"[582] the false penitent will ultimately have to concede that it was only the love of self that constrained him.

Why would anyone not endorse the blessing of discipleship to others, or even fail to pursue this blessing himself? Because discipleship is foolish to all who lack true saving faith which perceives the all-surpassing beauty of the Lord. It is a faithless Christianity that appeals to and promotes self. It is Christianity where the offence of the cross has ceased; where all that is difficult and unpleasant is removed, and where only that which is culturally relevant remains. It is a Christianity that seeks to advance Christianity, while abandoning the Christian worldview. This kind of Christianity easily sees the cross as the greatest manifestation of God's sacrificial love toward us, and this truth can never be overstated, but it fails to see Christ's call to take up the cross as a call to those who have experienced His love to sacrificially manifest it in return, and for no greater reason than their love for Him.

"Love is the greatest thing that God can give us," says Jeremy Taylor, "for He Himself is love; and it is the greatest thing we can give to God, for it will also give ourselves, and carry with it all that is ours."[583] Thomas Watson expressed the same sentiment when he wrote,

---

[581] Thomas Scott, *Letters and Papers of the Late Rev. Thomas Scott, D. D.* (Boston: Samuel T. Armstrong and Crocker and Brewster, 1825), 275.

[582] 2 Corinthians 5:14.

[583] Jeremy Taylor, *The Rules and Exercises of Holy Living and of Holy Dying* (Oxford and London: John Henry and James Parker, 1865; original, 1650), 189.

> Loving God evidences that God has the heart; and if the
> heart be His, that will command all the rest.[584]

Love must exist for faith to work. For Christ did not demonstrate His love toward us in order for us to demonstrate how much we love ourselves in our forsaking evil and following good. "He died for all, that those who live should live no longer for themselves, but for Him who died for them."[585] "Who His own self bare our sins in His own body on the tree, that we, being dead to sins, should live unto righteousness."[586] All must be false that is ultimately only consumed on self. For faith or love to be real, they must terminate in Him.

While faith and repentance are invaluable gifts from God, and indispensable means to Him, they are only valuable as they point to Christ, and ultimately end in Him. We must be careful that neither our faith nor repentance (as well as any other grace, ordinance, gift, spiritual exercise or experience) usurp His rightful place in the heart by becoming an end in itself. William Secker warns,

> I would neither have you be idle in the means, nor make
> an idol of the means.[587]

Faith has a high view of Christ and repentance a low view of sin, and thus of ourselves. It is in this capacity that they are invaluable. Faith obtains its value only as the indispensable means by which we receive Him who surpasses all value. It retains its value only so long as Christ remains its Object. The moment that faith turns from Him to trust in some other object, whether that object be ourselves, the church, our service, works or even in faith itself, it ceases to be faith, and serves no true purpose.

Our faith has no more merit before God than repentance or good works. It makes a world of difference whether we are resting in our faith or resting in the Author and Object of our faith. The moment we trust or

---

584 Thomas Watson, *A Divine Cordial* (Lafayette: Sovereign Grace Publishers), 2001; original, 1663), 67.

585 2 Corinthians 5:15.

586 1 Peter 2:24.

587 William Secker, *The Non-Such Professor in His Meridian Splendor* (New York: Fleming Revell, 1888), 161.

rest in our faith, we turn from Christ; therefore, we cannot trust or rest in some decision or prior act of faith, but must continually look to the Savior. While works evidences the reality of faith, they do not replace its Object. Faith justifies, not as a work that we perform, but as it lays hold of its Object. Thomas Goodwin gives the following warning,

> We put too much of our confidence upon signs, though true, and trust too much to our comforts and former revelations, and witnesses of God's Spirit, and to our graces, which are all but creatures [created things], acts of God upon us and in us. When therefore we let the weight of our support to hang on these, God, in this case, often leaves us, that no flesh should glory in His presence.[588]

Like Simeon, we must not rest satisfied by the fact that we are "just and devout,"[589] nor in our present level of spirituality ("the Holy Ghost was upon him,"[590] "revealed unto him by the Holy Ghost,"[591] "he came by the Spirit into the temple"),[592] but only in beholding Christ ("now lettest Thou Thy servant depart in peace....for my eyes have seen Thy Salvation").[593] Like him, we need an anti-consumer vision of Christ.

Since Christ is the all-absorbing Object of faith, all of the acts of faith must have an eye to Him. Whatever is performed while eyeing exclusively or primarily ourselves, man, or anything else, are merely acts of unbelief. Faith does not exist without an exchange of Object, from self, back unto God. Consumer-driven faith, therefore, is no faith at all, because its primarily object is the interests of the customer. "How can you believe who receive honor from one another, and do not seek the honor that comes from the only God."[594]

---

[588] Thomas Goodwin, *The Works of Thomas Goodwin, D. D.* Vol. III (Edinburgh: James Nichol, 1861), 293.

[589] Luke 2:25.

[590] Luke 2:25.

[591] Luke 2:26.

[592] Luke 2:27.

[593] Like 2:29,30.

[594] John 5:44.

Augustine said that "Christ is not valued at all unless He be valued above all."[595] If we are truly convinced of the reality of Christ, we would value Him above all else. And that which we value most, will have the greatest influence on our lives. Discipleship is an outward expression of the value of Christ whereby all those who are truly convinced of His claims, promises and realities, evidence their faith in a life of gracious obedience. All others will be little influenced by those things which they little believe, and therefore little esteem. True faith not only justifies, it also purifies[596] and produces obedience.[597] Therefore, to remove discipleship from the church is to strip it of its greatest expression and evidence of both faith and love for the One who gave Himself for her, and who now calls her, not only to glory,[598] but also to holiness,[599] and "from darkness to light."[600] All who proclaim this expression of both faith and love to be bondage, when it is actually glorious liberty, show their utter lack of either faith or love. They seek to make Christianity all about us, when it should be all about Him. A Christianity that is all about us naturally excludes Him from our lives altogether.

---

[595] Augustine, from *Westminster Collection of Christian Quotations* (Louisville: Westminster John Knox Press, 2001), 201.

[596] Acts 15:9.

[597] Romans 16:26.

[598] 1 Thessalonians 2:12.

[599] 1 Thessalonians 4:7.

[600] Ephesians 5:8.

CHAPTER 16

Faith Alters Life's Course by Exchanging Its Object

Again, the kingdom of heaven is like unto a merchant man, seeking goodly pearls; Who, when he had found one pearl of great price, went and sold all that he had, and bought it.

Matthew 13:45-46

The cost of discipleship corresponds with the worth of Christ. Does Christ ask too much of His disciples? He asks too much only if He is not all that the Scriptures declare Him to be. If He is all that the Scriptures claim He is, then He is infinitely worthy.[601] It is because of His infinite worthiness that our obligation to Him is infinitely binding. And because our obligation is infinitely binding, He asks little when He asks all.

Even if it were possible to live to Him perfectly, obeying all His will in every area of life, He would still not be indebted to us in any way, for we would have only done that which was not only our duty, but our highest delight. Rather it would be we who would be indebted to Him for the privilege of living wholly for Him. Therefore, the more holy we are, the more reason we should have for gratitude, and the humbler we should become. His worthiness turns duty into privilege. So, a clear grasp of the worthiness of Christ destroys at once both self-centeredness and

---

[601] Colossians 1:15 – 18; Revelations 5:9 – 13; 11:15 – 18.

self-righteousness. In other words, His worthiness not only implies that our discipleship deserves no thanks, since it, being imperfect, falls short of what God deserves, it also implies that our neglect of discipleship is infinitely evil. And those who exclude it from their ministry will be classed among those of whom Christ says, "depart from Me, ye that work iniquity."[602]

Discipleship will always be a hard pill to swallow for those who cherish the counterfeit offers of a consumer-driven Christianity above the preeminence of Christ, because the preference of these counterfeit offers always indicate a dissatisfaction with Christ. The Object of faith is only precious to the eye of faith. "To you who believe He is precious."[603] It is with the eye of faith that we perceive Christ's matchless beauty. This in turn inflames the heart to love and choose Him above all other objects. The real reason why consumer-driven Christianity will only promote a superficial discipleship, motivated by the superficial preferences of the consumer, is because self is still the exalted object in its eyes. We may accept the offer as precious, but unless Christ be found precious, He cannot be accepted. That faith cannot be saving which does not incline the will to prefer Him by first enkindling the affections to desire Him above all else; but only after it has been birthed in the soul by the Spirit through the Word which has revealed Him. Therefore, a heart to love God will always be in exact proportion to the degree of true saving faith. Alexander Maclaren observed that faith and love always exist together,

> Faith will obviously have for its certain and immediate consequence, love. Nay, the two emotions will be inseparable and practically co-existent. In thought we can separate them. Logically faith comes first, and love next, but in life they will spring up together. The question of their order of existence is an often-trod battle-ground of theology, all strewed with the relics of former fights. But in the real history of the growth of religious emotions in the soul the interval which separates them is impalpable, and in every act of trust

---

[602] Matthew 7:23.

[603] 1 Peter 2:7.

love is present, and fundamental to every emotion of
love to Christ is trust in Christ.[604]

Love is not the essence of faith, for they are two distinct virtues.[605]
But love is the proper and necessary outworking of faith. That which is the
result of something cannot be its essence. We are saved through faith, not
love, but we are saved through a faith that works by love.[606] Faith cannot
work properly without love. Faith that does not work by love, must receive
Him for reasons that are completely selfish. However legitimate, these
reasons may seem, devoid of love, they turn the soul entirely towards itself
in the very act of receiving, so that men, though seeming to turn toward
the Object of faith, are blinded by the overwhelming object of themselves.
But we will never receive Him while clenching ever so tightly to ourselves.

Love does not justify; it does not unite the soul to Christ in any saving
way. But it does, and must, unite the soul to Him in a practical way. Where
there is true saving faith in Christ, there will be true love for Christ. While
it is true that faith is the only saving grace, and unbelief the damning sin,
"he that believeth not shall be damned,"[607] as the fruit of faith, those who
lack love, also lack faith. Where good works do not exist, neither does
faith.[608] Since faith is inseparable from its fruits, it cannot exist where love
is not present. All works that are not motivated by love for God, then, do
not flow out of reconciliation, but from the lack thereof – the old nature.
As the fruit of faith, love becomes one of its evidences. How can I know
I have real faith? Simply ask, "how precious is Christ to me?" A saving
union cannot exist without a loving communion. It is because I find Him
precious, that I receive Him and endeavor to live for Him. Legalism is only
an option for those who find themselves precious and endeavor to live by
the power and for the glory of self. Lack of endeavor is not the cure. For
antinomianism is only an option for those who find themselves precious
and desire to live for themselves.

The act of saving faith is our receiving Him; believing cannot exist

---

[604] Alexander Maclaren, *Expositions on the Holy Scriptures* – The Acts (San
Diego: Icon Group International, 2008; reprint), 642.
[605] 1 Corinthians 13:13.
[606] Galatians 5:6.
[607] Mark 16:16.
[608] James 2:26.

without receiving. "As many as receive Him... even to those who believe in His name."[609] Faith is more than belief in certain facts about God, which is only an act of the intellect, it is also receiving and trusting in God, which is an act of the heart and will. "For with the heart one believes."[610] "If you believe with all your heart."[611] Although mental assent is essential, "for faith comes by hearing,"[612] and "how shall they believe in Him of whom they have not heard,"[613] it is not sufficient without the consent of the will to the assent of the intellect. William Guthrie explains,

> I grant, he that believeth on Jesus Christ believeth what God hath said concerning man's sinful, miserable condition by nature; and he believeth that to be true, that 'there is life in the Son, who was slain, and is risen again from the dead,' etc.: but none of these, nor the believing of many such truths, evidences justifying faith, or that believing on the Son of God spoken of in Scriptures; for then it were simply an act of the understanding; but true justifying faith, which we now seek after, as a good mark of an interest in Christ, is chiefly and principally an act or work of the heart and will; having presupposed sundry things about truth in the understanding.[614]

It is possible, then, for some to publicly acknowledge and accept the claims of Christ by human reason, who, through their lack of faith, are not fully persuaded of the reality of those claims. Saving faith is imparted by the Spirit, and is not a product of human persuasion, although always imparted by the Spirit through the means of human persuasion in the proclamation of the gospel. "And how shall they hear without a preacher?"[615] According to James Buchanan,

---

[609] John 1:12.

[610] Romans 10:10.

[611] Acts 8:37.

[612] Romans 10:17.

[613] Romans 10:14.

[614] William Guthrie, *The Christians Great Interest* (London: The Banner of Truth Trust, 1969; original, 1658), 62.

[615] Romans 10:14

there must be a subjective work of grace, in opening the blind eyes and making the light to shine into the heart, as well as an objective presentation of truth, in order to the production of true, spiritual, saving faith.[616]

William Guthrie writes,

Natural men, educated under gospel ordinances, although they have some notional knowledge of God, Christ, the promises, the motions of the Holy Spirit, etc., so that they may confer, preach, and dispute about these things; yet they look on them as common received maxims of Christianity from which to recede were a singularity and disgrace; but not as real, solid, substantial truths, so as to venture their souls and everlasting being on them.[617]

A.A. Alexander explains why this is the case,

And we see the reason why a merely rational, or historical faith does not work by love, nor produce any radical change in the character; because by it, however clear and strong, the excellence and beauty and glory of Christ and divine things are not revealed to the mind.[618]

It is an impossible task to persuade men to pay a high price for that which they esteem little in value. Hence the importance of communicating the value not only of the soul, but especially the beauty, glory and excellency of Christ in our preaching. For without a perception of His beauty, glory and excellency, no matter how high the performance or great the sacrifice, it will only be done for the beauty, glory and excellency we see in ourselves.

---

[616] James Buchanan, *Analogy Considered as a Guide to Truth and Applied as an Aid to Faith* (Edinburgh: Johnstone, Hunter and Co., 1864), 564.

[617] Guthrie, *Christians Great Interest*, 77.

[618] Archibald Alexander, *Practical Sermons to be Read in Family and Social Meetings.* (Philadelphia: Presbyterian Board of Publication, 1850), 21.

Those who are not truly convinced of the reality, nor see the beauty, of Christ, will give Him little influence in their lives. Whereas, those who are as fully persuaded by faith of His excellency, as Paul was,[619] will be as willing to suffer, sacrifice and risk all as he did.[620] None would venture so far for Christ as he did, who were not as fully convinced as he was. True faith involves the sacrifice of self as we live for Another; therefore, it will venture all and forsake all for Christ. Unbelief, on the other hand, will fashion a man-centered gospel where the stakes of our response to it are low. That which is man-centered will venture no further than where man is benefited. Hence, the rise of consumer-driven Christianity – a Christianity of little faith; a Christianity that allures, not by the brightness of His glory, but by the glory it bestows on self.

By faith Abraham left Ur, offered Isaac, and so ventured all at the call of God. Faith is more than, "I'll try God to see if it will benefit me, and if not, I'll try something else." It is a complete break with the past with no thought of looking back.[621] It is a complete surrender of self that is willing to risk all and lose all for Christ.[622] The surest way to judge the nature of your faith, then, is not by mental assent alone, but by the course of one's whole life, for one's life always reflects one's deepest convictions.

It is not sufficient to call men to receive His work on their behalf. Unless we receive Him for who He is, we only receive Him as a subordinate to some other object, namely self. While consumer-driven Christianity, by its very nature, calls men to self, for this is the real force behind its appeal, true conversion implies a turning from self. In conversion, we not only turn to Christ in faith, we also turn from all that is opposite to Him, or sets itself up in competition with Him, in repentance. Thus, we renounce all subordinate objects, including self. By this we judge a true from a false conversion.

Sin has not only clouded our understanding, it has disinclined our will. To say that faith includes an act of the will, excludes receiving Christ unwillingly in order to gain His benefits or avoid His wrath. The mind can reservedly choose Christ out of self-preservation, but the will can

---

[619] Philippians 2:16 – 17.

[620] Philippians 3:8.

[621] Luke 9:62.

[622] John 12:25.

only willingly choose Him out of desire. This, then, is not an act forced upon us because of self-love or fear of hell, but a willing choice based on Christ's own attractiveness. Therefore, we do not merely turn to Christ because our life is empty, and we hope to find new meaning in religion. Nor do we turn to Him solely out of self-preservation – "I don't want to go to hell." This requires nothing more than self-love and mental accent, and nothing supernatural.

"Whom have I in heaven but You?"[623] However desirable heaven is, Christ is more. Many will pass through the field without noticing the treasure. But there is only one response for the one who has found the treasure hidden therein, "for joy thereof goeth and selleth all that he hath, and buyeth that field."[624] They will joyfully receive that which they deem desirable and rejects that which they consider undesirable. Those who receive that which they deem undesirable merely for some other desirable end, still reject that as undesirable which they unwillingly receive.

It is with the will that we "believe on the Lord Jesus Christ."[625] We are not simply to believe Him and His gospel to be true. We are to believe "on Him." His call in the gospel is: "come onto Me."[626] "It is not merely a salvation, then, that Paul preaches," say B. B. Warfield, "but a Savior."[627] Therefore, none can receive Him who do not first find Him, and not just His offer, desirable. No one will trust in the words of anyone unless he first trusts the person who spoke the words. Therefore, there can be no trust in the gospel of Christ, without a trust in the Christ of the gospel.

> "To receive a guest is not to believe him to be my particular friend, though such he may be; but to open my doors to him, and make him heartily welcome. To receive an instructor is not to believe him to be my instructor any more than another's; but to embrace his instruction and follow his counsel. For a town, or city, after a long siege, to receive a king, is not to believe him

---

[623] Psalms 73:25.

[624] Matthew 13:44.

[625] Acts 16:31.

[626] Matthew 11:28.

[627] Benjamin B. Warfield, *The Power of God unto Salvation* (Grand Rapids: Eerdmans Publishing CO., 1930), 201.

> to be their special friend, though such he may be, and
> in the end, they may see it; but to lay down their arms,
> throw open their gates, and come under his government.
> These remarks are easily applied."[628]

Andrew Fuller

Although all the Word of God is the object of faith in a general sense, it is Christ, as presented in the Word, and enlightened by the Spirit, who is the particular Object of faith. There is an outward natural call and an inward spiritual call that is necessary before a saving response to the gospel is possible. Therefore, illumination is the necessary antecedent to faith. If faith is to set forth Christ as its Object, then Christ must be clearly set forth by the Word, through the Spirit, to the eye of faith.

If we are to receive Christ as the Word sets him forth, then we must receive Him like no other object. The tendency of focusing primarily on the understanding, and that only partially informed, while ignoring the will and affections, has led to multitudes of unaffected people deciding for Christ, while erroneously believing themselves to be Christians. The goal of evangelism is not to coerce a decision on the least amount of information possible (especially if the information only reinforces self-love), but to reveal the loveliness, desirableness, and suitableness of Christ that attracts men to Him, and compels a radical response. All who pretend to accept Christ and His benefits, then, but reject its indispensable link with discipleship, are blind to the loveliness of Christ that demands it, and thus find Him only partially attractive.

> "There can be no true religion, unless there is also a
> discovery of the real nature of God. But though there
> is a knowledge of what God is, unless there is also a
> discovery of the excellency and glory of His nature, He
> can never be the Object of esteem and love."[629]

John Witherspoon

---

[628] Andrew Fuller, *The Gospel Worthy of All Acceptation* (Boston: American Doctrinal Tract Society, 1846), 38.

[629] John Witherspoon, The Works of the Rev. John Witherspoon, Vol. I (Harrisonburg: Sprinkle Publications, 2001; original, 1801), 164.

"Come to Him by Christ, renounce the idols of your pleasure, gain, reputation. Let these be pulled from their throne, and set God's interest uppermost in your heart. Take Him as God, to be chief in your affections and purposes; for He will not endure to have any set above Him. In a word, you must take Him in all His personal relations and in all His essential perfections."[630]

Joseph Alleine

The questions of how one receives Christ, or whether one has truly received Him at all, are easily answered once we understand who He is that we receive. How do we receive Him? We can only receive Him for who He is, and all that He is, as set forth in the Word. Have we received Him? Only if we have received Him as the Word sets Him forth. True faith receives a whole Christ. While it may receive Him in any of His given offices at different times, it cannot reject any. If we do not receive Him as Master, thereby entering the path of discipleship, we have not received Him for who He is, and therefore have only secretly rejected Him even in the midst of our public profession of Him. "True faith receives Christ entire," says John Daggs, "as He is presented in the gospel. If any part of His character, of His offices, or of His doctrine is unwelcome to the heart, true faith does not dwell there."[631]

It is impossible, then, that any would reach out in faith to receive Him as Savior unless He were clearly set forth in the Word as Savior in all the freeness, fullness, and richness of His saving grace, mercy, and power. Likewise, it is impossible that any would receive Him as Lord, unless the Word had not so plainly set Him forth as the Lord, Sovereign, and Master, not only of the soul, but of all creation. The fact that Christ is so clearly and indisputably set forth in the Word in both roles indicates that in the same moment we receive Him as Savior, we must surrender to Him as Lord.[632] They are so essentially a part of His person that we cannot

---

[630] Joseph Alleine, *An Alarm to Unconverted Sinners* (Hanover: Charles Spear, 1816; original, 1671), 77

[631] John Daggs, *A Manuel of Theology* (Harrisonburg: Gano Books, 1990; original, 1857), 177.

[632] Colossians 2:6.

receive the one while ignoring the other. David Clarkson describes the impossibility of a partial acceptance of Christ when he writes,

> Many will take notice of Christ as a Savior, but not as Lord; but this is to take a view of Christ in an eclipse, to apprehend Christ without His crown. This is not to know Christ in all His discovered excellencies, and so is not the excellent knowledge of Christ.[633]

Edward Polhill confirms the same when he says,

> A sinner, whilst by his sinful rebellion, he strikes at His sovereignty or stabs at the holiness of God doth not, cannot, lean on free grace.... Faith is for all Christ; not for the meriting and atoning Christ only, but for a teaching and ruling one....a half Christ is not the Christ of God, but a Christ of his own fancy, such as cannot profit us....As to God, the ultimate Object, the believer would not pick and choose among His attributes, but is for them all.[634]

The debate of whether one can receive Christ as Savior, without receiving Him as Lord, is easily answered by those who have come to see Him for who He is. While faith is the hand that reaches out to receive, love is the heart of the new creature that finds the Object to be received desirable. It is in this sense that faith works by love, not only in our receiving Christ, but in all the proper actions of the new creature. It is inconceivable, then, how any can love Him as Savior while in practice rejecting Him as Sovereign, unless that same self-love that causes him to reject Him as Sovereign, also prompts him to receive Him as Savior. In other words, that same self-love that prompts him to receive Christ as Savior also causes him to reject Him as Lord.

---

[633] David Clarkson, *The Practical Works of David Clarkson*, Vol. I (Edinburgh: James Nichol, 1864), 251.
[634] Edward Polhill, *The Works of Edward Polhill* (Morgan: Soli Deo Gloria Publications, 1998; original, 1677), 245.

This, if possible, would be a very encouraging doctrine to the nominal believer, because it would allow him to believe that he has received the benefits of Christ, while remaining in an unregenerate state that is at enmity with the very essence of His Being. When the customer seeks a name to live, while remaining spiritually dead,[635] he merely seeks to ease his conscience with the hope of heaven even on the very path to hell. But if he could only lay aside his own predisposition towards himself, all his obligations to Christ would become obvious in the light of who Christ is. "The rights and claims of God," according to James Ramsey, "will be acknowledged, just in proportion as the perfections of His character are known and cherished."[636] The fact that these rights and claims are under attack today is because His perfections are less known and cherished. The solution lies not in multiplying more rules, but in magnifying Christ more.

Our partial appeals, directed towards the preferences of the customer, lead men to the religion of self, drawing them even further from God. The only reason we would receive an object that we did not love is because it carried along with it some other benefit that we do love. Many who do not like to study, work or exercise, do so every day merely to reap the benefits that accompany these actions. If the benefits were offered without these disciplines, many would neglect the disciplines to live a life of ease. A Christianity that promises the benefits without discipleship will be flooded with those who despise discipleship. This is the essence of consumer-driven Christianity. And its design and tendency is to fill the church with those who have no heart for God.

While God promises many benefits throughout Scripture relating to our obligations to Him, far from ignoring these benefits, we are commanded not to forget any of them.[637] But he who seeks God primarily for the benefits, only seeks himself, and reveals an utter lack of faith. John Flavel explains the reason why this is always the case,

---

[635] Revelation 3:1.

[636] James Ramsey, *The Book of Revelation* (Carlisle: The Banner of Truth Trust, 1995; original, 1873), 280.

[637] Psalms 103:2.

Christ and his benefits are inseparable. We can have no saving benefits apart from the person of Christ. Many would willingly receive His privileges who will not receive His person; but it cannot be: nay, we must accept His person first and then His benefits.[638]

Listen also to John Owen,

If we intend to have any benefit by Him, He must be valued above all for His own sake, or for the sake of what He is in Himself. He puts it as a mark upon them that follow Him, 'because of the loaves,' John 6:26. And if, without the knowledge of Christ, without a due consideration of His person, we think to follow Him only for His benefits, for the advantage which we hope to have by Him (which is to follow Him for the loaves), we shall be found strangers to Him, when we think we are in a better state and condition. Without this, no man can secure his love and faith from being selfish, or from beginning and ending in self. For if we regard only those things whereof we have advantage, so that we may have our sin pardoned, our iniquities done away, and our souls saved, we would not care whether there were a Christ to trust in or no. But as this tends not to the glory of God, so neither will it tend to the advantage of our own souls. So that if we intend any interest in Christ, we must begin with His person, and the knowledge of it.[639]

There can be no conversion where faith has not first brought about an awareness, not only of the greatness of our danger, and the greatness of our reward, but especially the all-surpassing greatness of Christ, the matchless Object of faith. Consumerism may attract many to Christianity where they can benefit from the goods, services, privileges,

---

[638] John Flavel, *The Method of Grace* (New York: American Tract Society), 16.
[639] John Owen, *The Works of John Owen D.D.* Vol. IX (London and Edinburgh: John Stone and Hunter, 1851), 478.

and ideas of the Christian marketplace, but it will never attract them to Christ, whose greatest attraction comes from who He is, and not merely from the benefits that accompany Him. However glorious, these benefits were only intended to enhance the alluring brightness of His glory, not to outshine it.

Printed in the United States
by Baker & Taylor Publisher Services